Person Re-identification with Limited Supervision

Synthesis Lectures on Computer Vision

Editor

Gérard Medioni, *University of Southern California*
Sven Dickinson *Samsung Toronto AI Research and University of Toronto*

Synthesis Lectures on Computer Vision is edited by Gérard Medioni of the University of Southern California and Sven Dickinson of the University of Toronto. The series publishes 50- to 150 page publications on topics pertaining to computer vision and pattern recognition. The scope follows the purview of premier computer science conferences, and includes the science of scene reconstruction, event detection, video tracking, object recognition, 3D pose estimation, learning, indexing, motion estimation, and image restoration. As a scientific discipline, computer vision is concerned with the theory behind artificial systems that extract information from images. The image data can take many forms, such as video sequences, views from multiple cameras, or multi-dimensional data from a medical scanner. As a technological discipline, computer vision seeks to apply its theories and models for the construction of computer vision systems, such as those in self-driving cars/navigation systems, medical image analysis, and industrial robots.

Image-Based Modeling of Plants and Trees
Sing Bing Kang and Long Quan
2009

Person Re-identification with Limited Supervision

Rameswar Panda and Amit K. Roy-Chowdhury

ISBN: 978-3-031-00697-5   paperback
ISBN: 978-3-031-01825-1   ebook
ISBN: 978-3-031-00082-9   hardcover

DOI 10.1007/978-3-031-01825-1

A Publication in the Springer series
SYNTHESIS LECTURES ON COMPUTER VISION

Lecture #18
Series Editors: Gérard Medioni, *University of Southern California*
                Sven Dickinson *Samsung Toronto AI Research and University of Toronto*
Series ISSN
Print 2153-1056   Electronic 2153-1064

Person Re-identification with Limited Supervision

Rameswar Panda and Amit K. Roy-Chowdhury
University of California, Riverside

SYNTHESIS LECTURES ON COMPUTER VISION #18

ABSTRACT

Person re-identification is the problem of associating observations of targets in different non-overlapping cameras. Most of the existing learning-based methods have resulted in improved performance on standard re-identification benchmarks, but at the cost of time-consuming and tediously labeled data. Motivated by this, learning person re-identification models with limited to no supervision has drawn a great deal of attention in recent years.

In this book, we provide an overview of some of the literature in person re-identification, and then move on to focus on some specific problems in the context of person re-identification with limited supervision in multi-camera environments. We expect this to lead to interesting problems for researchers to consider in the future, beyond the conventional fully supervised setup that has been the framework for a lot of work in person re-identification.

Chapter 1 starts with an overview of the problems in person re-identification and the major research directions. We provide an overview of the prior works that align most closely with the limited supervision theme of this book. Chapter 2 demonstrates how global camera network constraints in the form of consistency can be utilized for improving the accuracy of camera pair-wise person re-identification models and also selecting a minimal subset of image pairs for labeling without compromising accuracy. Chapter 3 presents two methods that hold the potential for developing highly scalable systems for video person re-identification with limited supervision. In the one-shot setting where only one tracklet per identity is labeled, the objective is to utilize this small labeled set along with a larger unlabeled set of tracklets to obtain a re-identification model. Another setting is completely unsupervised without requiring any identity labels. The temporal consistency in the videos allows us to infer about matching objects across the cameras with higher confidence, even with limited to no supervision. Chapter 4 investigates person re-identification in dynamic camera networks. Specifically, we consider a novel problem that has received very little attention in the community but is critically important for many applications where a new camera is added to an existing group observing a set of targets. We propose two possible solutions for on-boarding new camera(s) dynamically to an existing network using transfer learning with limited additional supervision. Finally, Chapter 5 concludes the book by highlighting the major directions for future research.

KEYWORDS

person re-identification, camera networks, limited supervision, network consistency, camera on-boarding, unsupervised learning

Contents

Preface

Person re-identification is a very fast-growing field of research. This book considers a specific aspect of this problem, i.e., how to learn re-identification models with limited supervision. This is related to research in machine learning on developing unsupervised to weakly supervised approaches, given the huge effort required in supervision. While the book tries to provide an overview of the work in this area, it does not claim to be an exhaustive review of every possible paper in a very fast-developing area of research. Rather, it focuses on a set of specific research directions in learning re-identification models with limited supervision. In order to highlight some of the research trends, the book identifies some specific topics of interest. These are chosen so as to lead the reader to increasingly complex ideas. First, we deal with the problem of how to minimize labeling effort in supervised approaches, followed by situations where the supervision is very limited, including one-shot supervision and unsupervised approaches. Thereafter, we consider the problem of dynamic camera networks where new camera(s) may be added or removed and show how learning-based approaches can be used in these settings, again with no to very limited supervision effort. There are many other directions that researchers should consider that are not described in detail in the book, and some of these are highlighted in the final chapter on future research directions.

We would like to thank a number of students in the Video Computing Group at UCR whose work over the years contributed to this book. They include Anirban Chakraborty, Abir Das, Niki Martinel, Sk Miraj Ahmed, Amran Bhuiyan, Sujoy Paul, Dripta Raychaudhuri, Sourya Roy, Xueping Wang, Shasha Li, and Abhishek Aich. They worked on related problems and published papers in top conferences and journals, creating a body of work that enabled this book. The authors would like to acknowledge support from the U.S. National Science Foundation, the U.S. Department of Defense and UC Riverside for their support through various grants for the work that led to this book. No monograph can do justice to a field that is evolving on a daily basis. However, we hope that the book will be valuable to researchers looking for a guide to the current state of the art and where the future challenges lie.

Rameswar Panda and Amit K. Roy-Chowdhury
August 2021

CHAPTER 1

Person Re-identification: An Overview

1.1   INTRODUCTION

Person re-identification (re-id for short), or more generally target re-identification, is the problem of associating observations of targets in different sensors (cameras in our case), usually with non-overlapping fields of view. Such associations are crucial for understanding a wide-area scene, which is likely to be observed by multiple cameras. It has its roots in classical data association methodologies like the Joint Probabilistic Data Association Filter [Fortmann et al., 1980], but has evolved significantly to deal with the challenges posed by visual data. Most current methods are deep learning-based, which has resulted in improved performance (compared to earlier approaches that did not use deep neural networks), but at the cost of time-consuming and tediously labeled data. More recently, the current trend in the field is to minimize such supervision without a sacrifice in the performance benefits. This book starts with an overview of the supervised learning-based approaches, and then discusses methods that aim to reduce the supervision. While the focus of this book is on person re-identification, the general ideas should be more broadly applicable to other kinds of targets, like vehicles [Huynh, 2021, Liu et al., 2016a,b, Zhou and Shao, 2018].

While target re-identification has been studied in various application scenarios, re-identification from video data has a number of challenges, stemming from the unique nature of videos. Observations of the same target may look very different in different sensors due to changes in lighting, occlusion, viewing direction, etc. This makes association very challenging. These challenges translate to learning-based approaches too. In order to mitigate these effects, the learned models need to have been trained with data that exhibit similar kinds of variations, which is often impossible due to the challenges of collecting and labeling data exhibiting all the different kinds of variations. Thus, it is necessary develop robust models for person re-identification with limited to no supervision.

The traditional learning-based approaches for person re-identification start with labeled data in each camera view. Considering pairs of cameras, a distance metric is learned that represents the transformation between the observed features in the cameras in each pair [Hirzer et al., 2012, Liao and Li, 2015a, Xing et al., 2002]. This requires learning the features to represent the objects, as well as learning the transformation metric between the cameras. This process needs to be repeated for each camera pair. For a large number of cameras, this simple approach is not scalable, and thus, it is necessary to develop other alternatives. One such alternative is to learn a global representation for the entire camera network [Liao et al., 2015a, Paisitkriangkrai et al., 2015a, Xiong et al., 2014], but this process may be problematic if there is a large variation in the observations across different cameras.

The drive to reduce supervision in the learning process has many dimensions, some of which are analyzed in this book. One of the questions we ask is whether there is an "optimal" level of supervision that would suffice for a particular setting. To answer this question, we first consider the re-identification problem in a global context of the entire network, where consistency checks between the matches in pairs of cameras are used to prune out erroneous matches. Thereafter, we use this idea to identify what is the minimal subset of targets that should be labeled and the consistency checks can be used to infer the labels of the other ones. We show that this can drastically reduce the labeling effort without sacrificing performance.

While an optimal subset of labeled data is very appealing, it may not be realistic in many settings, where the level of supervision is decided by the setup of the problem. We consider two such scenarios. In the one-shot setting where only one tracklet per identity is labeled, the objective is to utilize this small labeled set along with a larger unlabeled set of tracklets to obtain a re-identification model. In another, the setting is completely unsupervised without requiring any identity labels. In both of them, we consider re-id based on the video data, rather than single images. The temporal consistency in the videos allows us infer about matching objects across the cameras with higher confidence, even with limited to no supervision.

Toward the end of the book, we consider a novel problem that has received very little attention in the community but is critically important for many applications where cameras are mounted on mobile platforms. In this case, it is necessary to find associations between the targets in different cameras even as they move around. A completely supervised approach is not feasible since the camera configurations observing a related set of objects may change continuously. Thus, we could have a situation where a new camera is added to an existing group observing a set of targets, and this new camera needs to be integrated into the existing setup. We show how to address this problem of adding a new camera to an existing setup with limited to no additional supervision. We expect this to lead to interesting problems for researchers to consider in the future, beyond the static setup that has been the framework for almost all work in person re-identification.

Overall, this book provides an overview of some of the literature in person re-identification, and then moves on to focus on some specific problems of current interest. Learning from limited to no supervision is of interest in many machine learning applications [Roth, 2017, Van Engelen and Hoos, 2020, Xie et al., 2020, Yalniz et al., 2019, Zhou, 2018] and person re-identification is no exception. It has its unique challenges since the system needs to learn both the representative features, as well as the distance metrics. We provide a sampling of such approaches, which other researchers can build upon. We also introduce some of the challenges that would be encountered by cameras on mobile platforms, which will, hopefully, spur interest in this neglected aspect of the problem.

1.2   AN OVERVIEW OF RELATED WORK

Person re-identification has been studied from multiple perspectives (see Ye et al. [2021], Zheng et al. [2016b] for comprehensive reviews). Here, we provide an overview of the prior works that align most closely with the theme of this book: supervised re-identification, unsupervised re-id, semi-supervised and one-shot re-id, active learning for re-id, and open world person re-identification.

While multi-camera person re-identification, and by extension multi-camera tracking [Ristani et al., 2016, Ristani and Tomasi, 2018], is the most popular problem in camera networks that researchers are currently working on, it is not the only one. Another multi-camera problem that has been of interest to many is summarization, where the inter-camera correlations are used to identify redundancies that can improve the summarization results [Hussain et al., 2021, 2019, Panda et al., 2016, 2017b, Panda and Roy-Chowdhury, 2017]. Another problem of interest is active sensing where the cameras are controlled cooperatively so as to acquire images to meet the needs of different tasks, like some images at a higher resolution [Ding et al., 2016, 2012, Roy-Chowdhury and Song, 2012, Song et al., 2010]. Yet another interesting direction is distributed processing in a camera network where there is no central server where all the data is and decisions need to be based on communication among neighboring cameras and sharing limited information [Kamal et al., 2014, Song et al., 2011]. An interesting consensus algorithm for this purpose was proposed in Kamal et al. [2015, 2013]. In the future, it may be interesting to consider the re-id problem in conjunction with some of these aspects, e.g., re-identification in a distributed processing framework.

1.2.1   SUPERVISED PERSON RE-IDENTIFICATION

Most existing person re-identification techniques are based on supervised learning. These methods either seek the best feature representation [Bazzani et al., 2013a, Li et al., 2019a, Martinel et al., 2015, Wu et al., 2016] or learn discriminant metrics/dictionaries [Cao et al., 2019, Karanam et al., 2015, Koestinger et al., 2012, Liao et al., 2015b, Liao and Li, 2015b] that yield an optimal matching score between two cameras or between a gallery and a probe image.

Discriminative signature based methods [Bazzani et al., 2013a, Cheng et al., 2011, Liu et al., 2012, Martinel and Micheloni, 2012a] use multiple standard features e.g., color, shape, texture etc., or specially learned features like Biologically Inspired Features (BIF) [Ma et al., 2012], covariance descriptors [Bąk et al., 2012], shape descriptors of color distributions [Kviatkovsky et al., 2012], etc., to compute discriminative signatures for each person using multiple images.

Metric learning approaches focus on learning discriminant metrics which aim to yield an optimal matching score/distance between a gallery and a probe image. Since the early work of Xing et al. [2002], many different solutions have been introduced by relaxing [Hirzer et al.,

2012] or enforcing [Liao and Li, 2015a] positive semi-definite conditions as well as by considering equivalence constraints [Kostinger et al., 2012, Tao et al., 2014, 2013]. While most of the existing methods capture the global structure of the dissimilarity space, local solutions [García et al., 2016, Li et al., 2013, Pedagadi et al., 2013] have been proposed too. Following the success of both approaches, methods combining them in ensembles have also been introduced [Paisitkriangkrai et al., 2015a, Xiong et al., 2014]. In Liao et al. [2015c], authors jointly exploit the metric in Kostinger et al. [2012] and learn a low-rank projection onto a subspace with discriminative Euclidean distance. In Liao and Li [2015a], a soft-margin PSD constrained metric with low-rank projections is learned via a proximal gradient method. Both works exploit a batch optimization approach. Different solutions yielding similarity measures have also been investigated by proposing to learn listwise [Chen et al., 2015b] and pairwise [Zheng et al., 2013] similarities as well as mixture of polynomial kernel-based models [Chen et al., 2015a]. XQDA [Liao et al., 2015a] uses quadratic discriminant analysis to derive the metric. LMNN [Weinberger and Saul, 2009] learns the distance metric via penalizing closeness between dissimilar samples. The combination of triplet loss and identity loss is one of the most popular solutions for deep metric learning in person re-id [Guo et al., 2019, Guo and Cheung, 2018, Zhang et al., 2019b]. To further enrich the triplet supervision, a quadruplet deep network is also developed in Chen et al. [2017], where each quadruplet contains one anchor sample, one positive sample, and two mined negative samples. Network consistency is also utilized in Chakraborty et al. [2015] and Das et al. [2014] for increasing performance of camera pair-wise re-identification by re-organizing the predicted assignment matrix.

Both Gilbert and Bowden [2006] and Javed et al. [2008a] learned space-time probabilities of moving targets between cameras and used them as cues for association. In Avraham et al. [2012a], the re-identification problem was posed as a classification problem in the feature space formed of concatenated features of persons viewed in two different cameras. In Martinel and Micheloni [2015], the authors pose the re-identification problem as computing these nonlinear warp functions between features and learning a function space which models the feasible and the infeasible warp functions. Recently, deep learning methods have shown significant performance improvement on person re-id [Cheng et al., 2016, Lin et al., 2019b, Meng et al., 2019a, Yang et al., 2019, Yi et al., 2014, Zhou et al., 2018, 2017]. Combining feature representation and metric learning with end-to-end deep neural networks is also a recent trend in re-identification [Ahmed et al., 2015, Li et al., 2014, Luo et al., 2019]. Qian et al. [2017] developed a multi-scale deep representation learning model to capture discriminative cues at different scales.

Different attention schemes have also been widely studied in literature to enhance representation learning for person re-identification [Aich et al., 2021, Chen et al., 2019a, Li et al., 2018b, Yang et al., 2019, Zheng et al., 2019, Zhou et al., 2019]. A domain-guided dropout algorithm [Xiao et al., 2016] is designed to adaptively mine the domain-sharable and domain-specific neurons for multi-domain deep feature representation learning. In summary, these fully supervised methods have led to impressive progress in the field of re-id; however, it is impractical to annotate very large-scale surveillance data due to the dramatically increasing annotation cost.

1.2.2   UNSUPERVISED PERSON RE-IDENTIFICATION

Unsupervised learning models have recently received much attention in person re-id task as they do not require manually labeled data. Most of these methods alternatively assigning pseudo labels to unlabeled data with high confidence and updating the model using these pseudo-labeled data. While it is easy to collect unlabeled data in camera networks, most of these approaches perform weaker than supervised alternatives due to lack of efficient supervision.

Representative methods along this direction use either hand-crafted appearance features [Cheng et al., 2011, Liu et al., 2014a], saliency statistics [Zhao et al., 2013], or global network characteristics [Wang et al., 2020a] for matching persons without requiring huge amount of labeled data. Fan et al. [2018] proposed a k-means clustering-based method to select reliable images gradually and use them to fine tune a deep neural network to learn discriminative features for person re-id. Lin et al. [2019a] proposed a hierarchical clustering-based feature embedding method by regarding sample labels as supervision signals to train a nonparametric convolutional neural network [Xiao et al., 2017]. Liu et al. [2017] presented a person re-id method which iterates between cross-camera tracklet association and feature learning. Yu et al. [2019] proposed a soft multilabel learning method by comparing the unlabeled person images with a set of known reference person images from an auxiliary domain to predict the soft label for each target image. Li et al. [2018a] proposed a deep learning-based tracklet association method by jointly learning per-camera tracklet association and cross-camera tracklet correlation to obtain the label information. Zhong et al. [2019] exploited the underlying invariance in domain adaptive person re-id to reduce the feature distribution gap between labeled source domain and unlabeled target domain. Generative adversarial networks have also been adopted to train a camera style transfer model to bridge the gap between the labeled source domain and unlabeled target domain [Choi et al., 2018, Zhong et al., 2018].

Recently, several works also introduce graph matching into the person re-id task. Wu et al. [2019a] proposed an unsupervised graph association method to mine the cross-view relationships and reduce the damage of noisy associations. Ye et al. [2019] presented a dynamic graph co-matching method to obtain the corresponding image pairs across cameras. Lin et al. [2017] proposed a consistent-aware deep learning method by incorporating consistency constraints into deep learning framework for person re-id. The authors in Li et al. [2019b] utilize a camera aware loss by defining nearest neighbors across cameras being similar. Dictionary learning-based methods have also been utilized in an unsupervised setting [Kodirov et al., 2016]. Another line of research utilizes auxiliary datasets, which are completely labeled, for initializing a re-ID model and then using unsupervised domain adaptation techniques on the unsupervised target dataset.

1.2.3   SEMI-SUPERVISED AND ONE-SHOT PERSON RE-IDENTIFICATION

The limited performance of purely unsupervised methods [Chen et al., 2018, Lin et al., 2019a, Yu et al., 2017, 2019] has recently given rise to semi-supervised and one-shot methods in person re-identification. Some of the representative methods include dictionary learning [Liu et al., 2014b], graph matching [Hamid Rezatofighi et al., 2016], self-supervision [Raychaudhuri and Roy-Chowdhury, 2020], and metric learning [Bak and Carr, 2017]. Ye et al. [2017] use a dynamic graph matching strategy which iteratively updates the image graph and the label estimation to learn a better feature space with intermediate estimated labels. A stepwise metric learning approach to the problem is proposed in Liu et al. [2017]. Both these methods employ a static sampling strategy, where pseudo-labels with a confidence score above a pre-defined threshold are selected at each step, leading to a lot of noisy labels being incorporated in the learning process [Arazo et al., 2019].

In order to contain the noise, Wu et al. [2019b, 2018a] approach the problem from a progressive pseudo-label selection strategy, where the subset of the pseudo-labeled samples selected gradually increase with iterations. While this prevented the influx of noisy pseudo-labels, a significant portion of the unlabeled set is discarded at each step and thus, the unlabeled set is used inefficiently. Meng et al. [2019b] proposed a cross-view multiple instance multiple label learning method that exploits similar instances within a bag for intra-bag alignment and mine potential matched instances between bags. A recent work by Wang et al. [2021b] proposes a multiple instance attention learning framework for person re-identification using weak video-level labels. Specifically, the authors first cast the video person re-identification task into a multiple instance learning setting, in which person images in a video are collected into a bag. The relations between videos with similar labels are utilized to identify persons, with a co-person attention mechanism to mine the similarity correlations between videos with person identities that are common.

1.2.4   ACTIVE LEARNING FOR PERSON RE-IDENTIFICATION

In an effort to bypass tedious labeling of training data there has been interest in active learning [Settles, 2012] to intelligently select unlabeled examples for the experts to label in an interactive manner. Queries are selected for labeling such that enough training samples are procured in minimal effort. This can be achieved by choosing one sample at a time by maximizing the value of information [Joshi et al., 2012], reducing the expected error [Aodha et al., 2014], or minimizing the resultant entropy of the system [Biswas and Parikh, 2013]. Methods for selecting batches of unlabeled data by exploiting classifier feedback to maximize informativeness and sample diversity [Chakraborty et al., 2011, Elhamifar et al., 2013] were also proposed. Exploiting the structure in image or video data has also been shown to reduce the label queries in Hasan et al. [2018], Mithun et al. [2016], and Paul et al. [2017].

Active learning has been a relatively unexplored area in person re-identification [Das et al., 2015, Liu et al., 2013, 2019, Roy et al., 2018, Wang et al., 2016b, 2014]. These methods focused on post-ranking solutions and exploited human labor to refine the initial results by relying on full [Liu et al., 2013] or partial [Wang et al., 2014] image selection. Bai et al. [2017] propose a scalable re-id framework using manifold smoothing. Active learning is introduced for incremental updates in Wang et al. [2016a]. Das et al. [2015] introduce an entropy-based active learning strategy that exploits mid-level attributes to train a set of attribute predictors aiding active selection of images. Instead of relying on attributes, a temporal model adaptation approach with human in the loop for person re-identification is proposed in Martinel et al. [2016] using a graph-based solution that exploits the information provided by a single probe-gallery match as well as the information shared between all the persons in the entire gallery. With this, a small set of highly informative probe-gallery pairs is delivered to the human, whose effort is thus limited. A sparsity regularized convex optimization framework has been proposed in Das et al. [2017] to deal with non redundant representative selection, crucial to reducing the human labeling effort in a multi-camera setting through iterative active learning framework. The framework can, in general, be used for other multi-sensor active learning frameworks, e.g., activity recognition where data from multiple sensors may arrive in batches.

1.2.5 OPEN WORLD PERSON RE-IDENTIFICATION

Open world recognition was introduced in Bendale and Boult [2015] as an attempt to move beyond the static setting to a dynamic and open setting where the number of training images/classes are not fixed in recognition. Recently, there have been few works in person re-identification [Zheng et al., 2016c, Zhu et al., 2017] by assuming that gallery and probe sets contain different identities of persons. Multiple environmental constraints in dense crowds and social relationships are integrated for an open-world person re-id system in Assari et al. [2016]. Li et al. [2018c] introduce a deep open-world group-based person re-id model based on adversarial learning to alleviate the attack problem caused by similar non-target people. Cancela et al. [2014] consider associating persons observed in more than two cameras where different people can transit between different cameras so that there is only partial and unknown overlap of identity between people observed by each camera. Open world person re-identification using a drone on mobile platforms is presented in Layne et al. [2014]. A comprehensive survey on open world person re-identification can be found in Leng et al. [2019] and the total number of unique people among all cameras is itself unknown. Partial re-id which addresses the re-id problem with heavy occlusions is presented in He et al. [2018] and Zheng et al. [2015b]. Another important aspect of open world re-identification where the camera network is dynamic and the system has to incorporate a new camera with minimal additional effort is presented in Ahmed et al. [2020] and Panda et al. [2017a, 2019].

1.3   ORGANIZATION OF THE BOOK

This book provides a comprehensive review of the work done in the context of learning person re-identification models with limited to no supervision in multi-camera environments. The rest of the book is organized as follows.

In Chapter 2, we consider the problem of optimally selecting the minimal subset of data that needs to be labeled given a particular camera network and a set of observations. Specifically, we first demonstrate how global camera network constraints in form of consistency can be utilized for improving the accuracy of camera pair-wise person re-identification models and also selecting a minimal subset of image pairs for labeling without compromising accuracy.

Chapter 3 presents two methods that hold the potential for developing highly scalable systems for video person re-identification with limited supervision. In the first, we focus on one-shot video person re-id, where the objective is to utilize only one tracklet per identity along with a larger unlabeled set of tracklets for learning a re-id model. In the second, we aim to develop a fully unsupervised solution by exploiting global network characteristics that does not require any identity labels.

Chapter 4 investigates person re-identification in dynamic camera networks. We propose two possible solutions for on-boarding new camera(s) dynamically to an existing network using transfer learning with limited additional supervision. First, we develop an unsupervised framework that can effectively discover and transfer knowledge from the best source camera (already installed) to a newly introduced target camera(s), without requiring a very expensive training phase. Second, we propose an efficient multiple metric hypothesis transfer learning algorithm to efficiently adapt a newly introduced camera to an existing framework using only source models and limited labeled data without having access to the source data.

Chapter 5 provides a vision for future research directions, including knowledge transfer across networks, adversarial robust re-identification, efficient model deployment in resource-limited applications, human-in-the-loop re-identification, and adversarial attacks on re-identification systems.

CHAPTER 2

Supervised Re-identification: Optimizing the Annotation Effort

Supervised distance metric learning-based methods for person re-id are specifically popular because of their robustness toward large color variations and fast training speed. However, like other supervised methods, metric learning algorithms have their own burden of human labeling effort especially for large camera networks. The total number of training pairs assumed to be available by these algorithms increases tremendously with network size and number of persons in each camera. Manual labeling of such huge number of pairs is a tedious and expensive process. So, naturally a question arises: given a camera network, *can we come up with a strategy of choosing a minimal subset of image pairs for labeling without compromising on recognition performance?* This is a problem of considerable significance in the context of person re-id in multi-camera networks, especially in larger ones.

In this chapter, we consider the problem of optimally selecting the minimal subset of data that needs to be labeled given a particular camera network and a set of observations. We achieve this by considering the *global* characteristics of the camera network, which we term as *network consistency*. For the purposes of a clear explanation, we first show how to improve the camera pairwise re-identification performance by considering network consistency, and then show how to minimize the manual labeling effort in re-identification by selecting an optimal subset of image-pairs for labeling without compromising performance. Thus, we first propose a network-consistent re-identification framework where the resulting optimization problem is translated into a binary integer program which can be solved using standard branch and cut, branch and bound, or dynamic search algorithms, leading to a globally optimal solution [Chakraborty et al., 2015, Das et al., 2014]. Second, we develop a pairwise subset selection framework by leveraging transitive relations to minimize human labeling effort for person re-id in camera networks [Roy et al., 2018].

2.1 NETWORK CONSISTENT RE-IDENTIFICATION

Most existing person re-identification methods focus on finding similarities between persons between pairs of cameras (camera pairwise re-identification) without explicitly maintaining con-

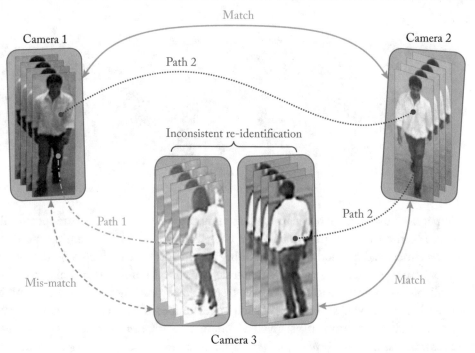

Figure 2.1: Example of network inconsistency in person re-identification: Among the three possible re-identification results, two are correct. A match of the target from camera 1 to camera 3 can be found in two ways. The first one is the direct pairwise re-identification result between cameras 1 and 3 (shown as "Path 1"), and the second one is the indirect re-identification result in camera 3 given via the matched person in camera 2 (shown as "Path 2"). The two outcomes do not match and thus the overall associations of the target across three cameras is not consistent. Best viewed in color.

sistency of the results across the network. Matches between targets given independently by every pair of cameras might not conform to one another and, in turn, may lead to inconsistent mappings. Thus, in person re-identification across a camera network, multiple paths of correspondences may exist between targets from any two cameras, but ultimately all these paths must point to the same correspondence maps for each target in each camera. An example scenario is shown in Fig. 2.1. Even though camera pairs 1-2 and 2-3 have correct re-identification of the target, the false match between the targets in camera pair 1-3 makes the overall re-identification across the triplet inconsistent. It can be noted that the error in re-identification manifests itself through inconsistency across the network, and hence by enforcing consistency the pairwise accuracies can be improved as well.

To achieve a consistent and optimal re-identification, we pose the problem of re-identification as an optimization problem that minimizes the global cost of associating pairs of targets on the entire camera network constrained by a set of consistency criteria. The pairwise re-identification similarity scores obtained using any feasible approach are the input to the proposed method. Unlike assigning a match for which the similarity score is maximum among a set of probable candidates, our formulation picks the assignments for which the total similarity of all matches is the maximum, as well as the constraint that there is no inconsistency in the assignment among any pair of cameras given any other intermediate camera. The resulting optimization problem is translated into a binary integer program (IP) which can be solved using standard branch and cut, branch and bound, or dynamic search algorithms [Schrijver, 1998]. The application of the proposed formulation is not limited only to person re-identification, but can also be applied in solving other correspondence problems between multiple nodes/instances arising out of the same object at different instants, e.g., object tracking, optical flow, feature correspondences, etc.

2.1.1   ESTIMATING GLOBALLY CONSISTENT ASSOCIATIONS

The Network Consistent Re-identification (NCR) method starts with the camera pairwise similarity scores between the targets. Let there be m cameras in a network. The number of possible camera pairs is $\binom{m}{2} = \frac{m(m-1)}{2}$. For simplicity we, first, assume, that the same n person are present in each of the cameras. However, our approach can be easily extended for a variable number of targets.

Node and Similarity Score Matrix. The ith person in camera p is denoted as $\mathcal{P}_i^p$ and is called a "node" in this framework. Let $\mathbf{C}^{(p,q)}$ denote the similarity score matrix between camera p and camera q. Then (i, j)th cell in $\mathbf{C}^{(p,q)}$ denotes the similarity score between the persons $\mathcal{P}_i^p$ and $\mathcal{P}_j^q$.

Assignment Matrix. The associations between targets across cameras can be represented using "assignment matrices," one for each camera pair. Each element $x_{i,j}^{p,q}$ of the assignment matrix $\mathbf{X}^{(p,q)}$ between the camera pair (p, q) is defined as follows:

$$x_{i,j}^{p,q} = \begin{cases} 1 & \text{if } \mathcal{P}_i^p \text{ and } \mathcal{P}_j^q \text{ are the same targets} \\ 0 & \text{otherwise.} \end{cases} \tag{2.1}$$

As a result, $\mathbf{X}^{(p,q)}$ is a permutation matrix, i.e., only one element per row and per column is 1, all the others are 0. Mathematically, $\forall\, x_{i,j}^{p,q} \in \{0, 1\}$

$$\sum_{j=1}^{n} x_{i,j}^{p,q} = 1\ \forall i = 1 \text{ to } n \text{ and } \sum_{i=1}^{n} x_{i,j}^{p,q} = 1\ \forall j = 1 \text{ to } n. \tag{2.2}$$

Edge and Path. An "edge" between two nodes $\mathcal{P}_i^p$, and $\mathcal{P}_j^q$ from two different cameras is a probable association between i^{th} person in camera p and jth person in camera q. There are two attributes connected to each edge. They are the similarity score $c_{i,j}^{p,q}$ and the association value $x_{i,j}^{p,q}$. Similarly, a "path" between two nodes $(\mathcal{P}_i^p, \mathcal{P}_j^q)$ is a set of edges that connect $\mathcal{P}_i^p$ and $\mathcal{P}_j^q$ without traveling through a camera twice. A path between $\mathcal{P}_i^p$ and $\mathcal{P}_j^q$ can be represented as the set of edges $e(\mathcal{P}_i^p, \mathcal{P}_j^q) = \{(\mathcal{P}_i^p, \mathcal{P}_a^r), (\mathcal{P}_a^r, \mathcal{P}_b^s), \ldots (\mathcal{P}_c^t, \mathcal{P}_j^q)\}$, where $\{\mathcal{P}_a^r, \mathcal{P}_b^s, \ldots \mathcal{P}_c^t\}$ are the set of intermediate nodes on the path between $\mathcal{P}_i^p$ and $\mathcal{P}_j^q$. The set of association values on all the edges between the nodes is denoted as $\mathcal{L}$, i.e., $x_{i,j}^{p,q} \in \mathcal{L}$, $\forall i, j = [1, \ldots, n]$, $\forall p, q = [1, \ldots, m]$ and $p < q$. Finally, the set of all paths between any two nodes $\mathcal{P}_i^p$ and $\mathcal{P}_j^q$ is represented as $\mathcal{E}(\mathcal{P}_i^p, \mathcal{P}_j^q)$ and any path $e^{(z)}(\mathcal{P}_i^p, \mathcal{P}_j^q) \in \mathcal{E}(\mathcal{P}_i^p, \mathcal{P}_j^q)$.

Global Similarity of Association. For the camera pair (p, q), the sum of the similarity scores of association is given by $\sum_{i,j=1}^{n} c_{i,j}^{p,q} x_{i,j}^{p,q}$. Summing over all possible camera pairs the global similarity score can be written as

$$C = \sum_{\substack{p,q=1 \\ p<q}}^{m} \sum_{i,j=1}^{n} c_{i,j}^{p,q} x_{i,j}^{p,q}. \tag{2.3}$$

Association Constraint. A person from any camera p can have only one match from another camera q. This is mathematically expressed by the set of Eqs. (2.2). This is true for all possible pairs of cameras which can be expressed as

$$\sum_{j=1}^{n} x_{i,j}^{p,q} = 1 \ \forall i = 1 \text{ to } n \ \forall p, q = 1 \text{ to } m, \ p < q$$

$$\sum_{i=1}^{n} x_{i,j}^{p,q} = 1 \ \forall j = 1 \text{ to } n \ \forall p, q = 1 \text{ to } m, \ p < q. \tag{2.4}$$

Loop Constraint. This constraint comes from the consistency requirement. Given two nodes $\mathcal{P}_i^p$ and $\mathcal{P}_j^q$, it can be noted that, for consistency, a logical "AND" relationship between the association value $x_{i,j}^{p,q}$ and the set of association values $\{x_{i,a}^{p,r}, x_{a,b}^{r,s}, \ldots x_{c,j}^{t,q}\}$ of a possible path between the nodes has to be maintained. The association value between the two nodes $\mathcal{P}_i^p$ and $\mathcal{P}_j^q$ has to be 1 if the association values corresponding to all the edges of any possible path between these two nodes are 1. Keeping the binary nature of the association variables and the association constraint in mind the relationship can be compactly expressed as

$$x_{i,j}^{p,q} \geq \left(\sum_{(\mathcal{P}_k^r, \mathcal{P}_l^s) \in e^{(z)}(\mathcal{P}_i^p, \mathcal{P}_j^q)} x_{k,l}^{r,s} \right) - |e^{(z)}(\mathcal{P}_i^p, \mathcal{P}_j^q)| + 1, \tag{2.5}$$

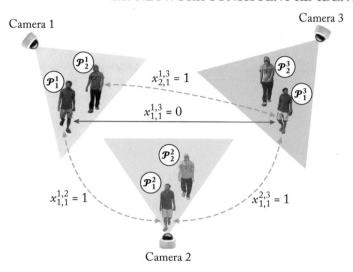

Figure 2.2: An illustrative example showing that inconsistent re-identification is captured by the loop constraint given by Eq. (2.6) for a simple scenario involving two persons in three cameras.

$\forall$ paths $e^{(z)}(\mathcal{P}_i^p, \mathcal{P}_j^q) \in \mathcal{E}(\mathcal{P}_i^p, \mathcal{P}_j^q)$, where $|e^{(z)}(\mathcal{P}_i^p, \mathcal{P}_j^q)|$ denotes cardinality of path $|e^{(z)}(\mathcal{P}_i^p, \mathcal{P}_j^q)|$, i.e., number of edges in the path. The relationship holds true for all i and all j. For the case of a triplet of cameras the constraint in Eq. (2.5) simplifies to

$$x_{i,j}^{p,q} \geq x_{i,k}^{p,r} + x_{k,j}^{r,q} - 2 + 1 = x_{i,k}^{p,r} + x_{k,j}^{r,q} - 1. \tag{2.6}$$

An example involving three cameras and two persons is illustrated with the help of Fig. 2.2. Say that, the raw similarity score between pairs of targets across cameras suggests associations between $(\mathcal{P}_1^1, \mathcal{P}_1^2)$, $(\mathcal{P}_1^2, \mathcal{P}_1^3)$, and $(\mathcal{P}_2^1, \mathcal{P}_1^3)$ independently. However, when these associations are combined together over the entire network, it leads to an infeasible scenario—$\mathcal{P}_1^1$ and $\mathcal{P}_2^1$ are the same person. This infeasibility is also correctly captured through the constraint in Eq. (2.6). $x_{1,1}^{1,3} = 0$ but $x_{1,1}^{1,2} + x_{1,1}^{2,3} - 1 = 1$, thus violating the constraint. For a generic scenario involving a large number of cameras where similarity scores between every pair of cameras may not be available, the loop constraint equations (i.e., Eq. (2.5)) have to hold for every possible triplet, quartet, quintet (and so on) of cameras. On the other hand, if the similarity scores between all persons for every possible pair of cameras are available, the loop constraints on quartets and higher order loops are not necessary. If loop constraint is satisfied for every triplet of cameras then it automatically ensures consistency for every possible combination of cameras taking three or more of them. So, the loop constraint for the network of cameras becomes,

$$x_{i,j}^{p,q} \geq x_{i,k}^{p,r} + x_{k,j}^{r,q} - 1$$
$$\forall\, i, j = [1, \ldots n], \; \forall\, p, q, r = [1, \ldots m], \text{ and } p < r < q. \tag{2.7}$$

Overall Optimization Problem.   Thus, by combining the objective function in Eq. (2.3) with the constraints in Eq. (2.4) and Eq. (2.7), we pose the overall optimization problem as follows:

$$\underset{\substack{x_{i,j}^{p,q} \\ i,j=[1,\dots,n] \\ p,q=[1,\dots,m]}}{\mathrm{argmax}} \left(\sum_{\substack{p,q=1 \\ p < q}}^{m} \sum_{i,j=1}^{n} c_{i,j}^{p,q} x_{i,j}^{p,q} \right)$$

$$\text{subject to } \sum_{j=1}^{n} x_{i,j}^{p,q} = 1 \ \forall i = [1,\dots,n] \ \forall p,q = [1,\dots,m], \ p < q$$

$$\sum_{i=1}^{n} x_{i,j}^{p,q} = 1 \ \forall j = [1,\dots,n] \ \forall p,q = [1,\dots,m], \ p < q$$

$$x_{i,j}^{p,q} \geq x_{i,k}^{p,r} + x_{k,j}^{r,q} - 1$$

$$\forall i,j = [1,\dots n], \ \forall \ p,q,r = [1,\dots m], \ \text{and} \ p < r < q$$

$$x_{i,j}^{p,q} \in \{0,1\} \ \forall i,j = [1,\dots,n], \ \forall p,q = 1 \text{ to } m, \ p < q.$$

(2.8)

The above optimization problem for optimal and consistent re-identification is a binary integer program.

2.1.2   EXAMPLES OF GLOBALLY CONSISTENT RE-IDENTIFICATION

Dataset and Settings. To validate our approach, we performed experiments on WARD [Martinel and Micheloni, 2012b] dataset which contains 4786 images of 70 different people acquired in a real surveillance scenario in 3 non-overlapping cameras (see Fig. 2.3 for few sample images). The 70 people in this dataset are equally divided into training and test sets of 35 persons each. Results are shown in terms of recognition rate as Cumulative Matching Characteristic (CMC) curves which is a plot of the recognition percentage vs. the ranking score and represents the expectation of finding the correct match inside top t matches. The camera pairwise similarity score generation starts with extracting appearance features in the form of HSV color histogram from the images of the targets. We then generate the similarity scores by learning the way features get transformed between cameras in a similar approach as Javed et al. [2008b]. Specifically, instead of using feature correlation matrix or the feature histogram values directly, we capture the feature transformation by warping the feature space in a nonlinear fashion inspired by the principle of Dynamic Time Warping. In addition to a feature transformation-based method, similarity scores are also generated using ICT [Avraham et al., 2012b] where pairwise re-identification was posed as a classification problem in the feature space formed of concatenated features of persons viewed in two different cameras. For each test we ran five independent trials and report the average results.

Figure 2.3: Six image pairs from the WARD dataset. Columns correspond to different persons, rows to different cameras. As seen from the figure, person re-identification in this dataset is a challenging problem due to viewpoint changes, occlusions, illumination changes, and background clutter in images of the same person in cameras with non-overlapping fields of view. Best viewed in color.

Baselines. The proposed approach is compared with the methods SDALF [Bazzani et al., 2013b], ICT [Avraham et al., 2012b], and WACN [Martinel and Micheloni, 2012b]. The legends "NCR on FT" and "NCR on ICT" imply that our NCR algorithm is applied on similarity scores generated by the feature transformation and ICT, respectively.

Results. Figure 2.4 shows the results. For all three camera pairs the proposed method outperforms the rest. The difference is most clear in the rank 1 performance. For all the camera pairs, "NCR on FT" shows the best rank 1 performance of recognition percentages as high as 57.14, 45.15, and 61.71 for camera pairs 1-2, 1-3, and 2-3, respectively. The runner up in camera pair 1-2 is "NCR on ICT" with rank 1 recognition percentage of 40. The runner up for the rest of the camera pairs is "FT" with corresponding numbers for camera pairs 1-3 and 2-3 being 35.43 and 50.29, respectively. Figure 2.5 shows two example scenarios from this dataset where inconsistent re-identifications are corrected on application of the NCR algorithm.

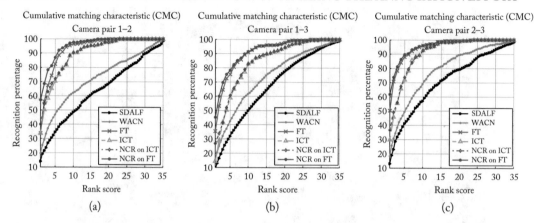

Figure 2.4: CMC curves for WARD dataset. Results and comparisons in (a), (b), and (c) are shown for camera pairs 1-2, 1-3, and 2-3, respectively. Best viewed in color.

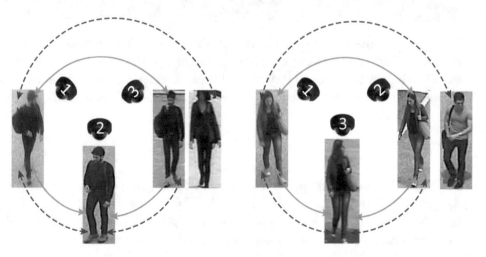

Figure 2.5: Two examples of correction of inconsistent re-identification from the WARD dataset. The red dashed lines denote re-identifications performed on three camera pairs independently by the FT method. The green solid lines show the re-identification results on application of NCR on FT. The NCR algorithm exploits the consistency requirement and makes the resultant re-identification across three cameras correct.

2.2   OPTIMAL SUBSET SELECTION FOR ANNOTATION

Having studied the problem of NCR and how global consistency can be enforced to improve the accuracy of person re-id, we now focus on another related problem. Can we use the idea of global network consistency to drastically reduce the supervision effort and identify an optimal subset of data to label? We hypothesize that transitive or consistency relations among person identities across multiple cameras and their logical consequences are strongly informative properties for reducing the labeling effort. Building upon the description above, which explored these properties for globally consistent person re-id [Chakraborty et al., 2016, Das et al., 2014], we now show how to exploit the transitive relations to reduce manual pairwise annotation effort. To illustrate the idea, let us consider a few plausible scenarios, as shown in Fig. 2.6a.

- In camera pair 1-2 and 1-3, if we know from human labeling person that pairs $P_1^1 - P_2^1$ and $P_1^1 - P_3^2$ are positive matches, then from transitivity we can directly infer that P_2^1 and P_3^2 also have same identity. Similarly, given labels of $P_1^1 - P_2^1$ (+ve) and $P_1^1 - P_3^1$ (−ve), we can infer that $P_2^1 - P_3^1$ is negative.

- However, given that we already know labels of $P_1^1 - P_2^2$ (−ve) and $P_1^1 - P_3^1$ (−ve), we still cannot conclude anything about pair $P_2^2 - P_3^1$.

So, from the examples above we can make a simple observation, i.e., if we do not ask an expert for the label of the third pair/s in the first two cases described above, required labeling effort will be considerably reduced. However, this seemingly simple strategy implicitly makes an invalid assumption that we already have access to the pair-labels from human. Also, note that if we arbitrarily choose subsets of pairs for labeling there is no guarantee that we will be able to take advantage of pairwise-relations as we will end up frequently in situations like the third scenario (occurrence probability of this scenario is significantly higher than the other two). So, in order to actually reduce annotation effort using this transitivity based approach, we have to choose image pairs in a judicious manner.

Towards this objective, we first formulate this pair subset selection as a combinatorial optimization problem on edge-weighted k-partite graph. This combinatorial optimization can be represented as a binary integer program which we can solve exactly for smaller datasets using standard techniques such as branch and cut [Mitchell, 2002], cutting plane algorithms [Marchand et al., 2002], etc. However, as it is an NP-hard optimization problem, solving it with exact algorithms takes exponential order time and for larger datasets it becomes intractable. So, in order to scale up the proposed methodology for large camera networks, we propose two polynomial-time sub-optimal algorithms for our optimization problem. The first one is a pure greedy algorithm and second one is a 1/2-approximation algorithm [Roy et al., 2018].

2.2.1   ESTIMATING THE OPTIMAL SUBSET

We represent any camera network as a edge weighted complete k-partite graph $G_k = (V, E)$ (see Fig. 2.6b). Below we describe how this partite graph is constructed from a camera network consisting of k cameras and total n persons across all cameras.

Vertex and Edges. Each vertex in G_k denotes a person in the camera network. To be precise, vertex $v_{k'}^i$ represents the ith person from k'th camera. From now on, throughout rest of the work we will use the terms "person" and "vertex" interchangeably. An edge $E_{k_1,k_2}^{i,j} = (v_{k_1}^i, v_{k_2}^j)$

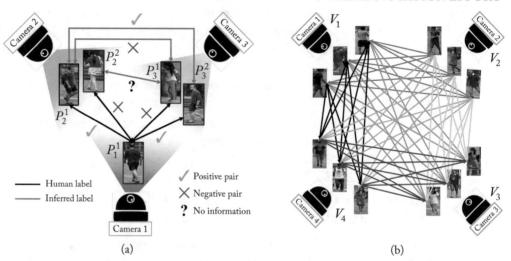

Figure 2.6: (a) Motivation of our approach. Here, we have a camera network with three cameras. P_k^i represent the "i"th person in the "k"th camera. Now, suppose we ask the human to label the pairs $P_1^1 - P_2^1$ and $P_1^1 - P_3^2$ by asking a yes/no question. As both of them are positive matches, after we know the labels of these two pairs using transitivity property we can correctly infer the label of $P_2^1 - P_3^2$. Similarly, if we know labels of $P_1^1 - P_2^1$ and $P_1^1 - P_3^1$ we can precisely infer that $P_2^1 - P_3^1$ is a negative match. However, knowing the labels of pairs $P_1^1 - P_2^2$ and $P_1^1 - P_3^1$ does not give us any information about the pair $P_2^2 - P_3^1$. (b) Network Representation. This figure demonstrates representation of a camera network with four cameras as a k-partite graph with $k = 4$.

denotes probable correspondence between ith person in camera k_1 and jth person in camera k_2.

Vertex Set Partitions. As per our definition, the set of all the persons in a camera network forms the vertex set V of G_k. Now in our framework, we assume the intra-camera vertices are not connected to each other, i.e., they form an independent vertex set. So, k sets of vertices from each different camera form k different partitions. More formally, $V = (V_1, V_2, ..., V_k)$ where $V_{k'} = \{v_{k'}^1, v_{k'}^2, ..., v_{k'}^{n_{k'}}\}$ is the set of $n_{k'}$ persons in k'th camera. So, if we have $n_1, n_2, ..., n_k$ persons in camera 1, camera 2, ..., camera k, respectively, the cardinality of the set V is

$$|V| = \sum_{i=1}^{k} |V_i| = n_1 + n_2 + \cdots + n_k = n. \tag{2.9}$$

Now, G_k is a complete multipartite graph as we have probable correspondences (i.e., an weighted edge) between every pair of vertices from different partitions. So the total number of edges in the graph, can be computed as follows:

$$|E| = \sum_{\substack{\forall k_1 \in \{1,2,...,k\} \\ \forall k_2 \in \{1,2,...,k\} \\ s.t. \ k_1 < k_2}} n_{k_1} n_{k_2}.$$ (2.10)

Edge Weight. We define our edge weight function $\mathcal{F}_w : E \to \mathbb{R}$, as follows:

$$\mathcal{F}_w\big(E^{i,j}_{k_1,k_2}\big) = \mathcal{S}\big(v^i_{k_1}, v^j_{k_2}\big),$$ (2.11)

where $\mathcal{S}$ is a function which computes similarity or association score between two persons $v^i_{k_1}$ and $v^j_{k_2}$. Note that our framework can be used with any kind of similarity measure. As we define our objective function later over non-negative edge weights, the proposed scheme will scale any negative valued similarity score into a non-negative value using the sigmoid function. In this work, we compute similarity scores between a pair of shots of two persons as follows:

$$\mathcal{S}\big(v^i_{k_1}, v^j_{k_2}\big) = \frac{1}{1 + \exp\big(\mathcal{D}(f^i_{k_1}, f^j_{k_2}) - \mu\big)},$$ (2.12)

where $f^i_{k_1}, f^j_{k_2}$ are feature vectors of corresponding persons $v^{k_1}_i, v^{k_2}_j$, respectively, $\mathcal{D}$ is a distance function giving distance between two feature vectors, and μ is a threshold.

Triangle. Complete subgraphs (or clique) of size 3 are referred to as a triangle in any graph. Naturally, whenever we have three persons(vertices), $v^i_{k_1}, v^j_{k_2}, v^l_{k_3}$ from three different cameras (camera k_1, camera k_2, and camera k_3), they form a triangle, $T^{i,j,l}_{k_1,k_2,k_3} = \big\{v^i_{k_1}, v^j_{k_2}, v^l_{k_3}\big\}$. As we progress, we will see that triangles are the central objects around which our whole framework evolves.

With the initial setup in place, we can now formulate the image pair selection task as an optimization problem on our graph G_k. Let us consider first revisiting the problem statement of the budget constrained pair-selection task.

Optimization Problem.   Given a labeling budget, B, and a set of training image pairs from a camera network, we have to select an optimal subset of size at most B for human annotation. The notion of "optimal subset" is *incomplete*. As seen from Fig. 2.6a, the transitive relations defined over associations between different persons (vertices) can be utilized for labeling effort reduction. Now we give that idea a concrete shape by making some specific observations in the context of our graph G_k.

- For any triangle in our graph, we have a total three edges from which we can select for manual labeling.

- We may always want to select positive edges as they will contribute more toward reducing manual labeling effort because transitive inference in our graph always requires at least one positive edge.

- As shown in Fig. 2.6, if we have precise information about two edges in a triangle of our graph, and one of them is a positive edge then we can deterministically infer the label of the third edge. For this reason we must always want to constrain the number of edges chosen for manual labeling in a triangle be at most two in order to respect the budget.

- As we cannot foresee actual labels, we have to choose that pair of edges from any triangle which will maximize probability of getting at least one positive match.

- Also, note that any edge is a part of multiple triangles in our graph, so inference propagation can occur from different directions.

With these observations in mind, our optimization problem can be stated as:

- *Given a complete k-partite graph $G_k = (V, E)$ with non-negative edge weights and an integer B, choose a maximum-weight set S of edges from E such that $G' = (V, S)$ is triangle free and $|S| \leq B$.*

An Equivalent Binary Integer Program. Our combinatorial optimization can be formulated as a binary integer programing problem as follows:

$$\underset{\substack{x_{k_1,k_2}^{i,j} \\ \forall (i,j) \in \delta(k_1,k_2) \\ \forall k_1,k_2 \in \{1,\ldots,k\} \, s.t \, k_1 < k_2}}{\operatorname{argmax}} \left(\sum_{\substack{k_1,k_2=1 \\ k_1 < k_2}}^{k} \sum_{i,j=1}^{n_{k_1},n_{k_2}} w_{k_1,k_2}^{i,j} x_{k_1,k_2}^{i,j} \right) \tag{2.13}$$

$$\text{subject to: } \sum_{\substack{k_1,k_2=1 \\ k_1 < k_2}}^{k} \sum_{i,j=1}^{n_{k_1},n_{k_2}} x_{k_1,k_2}^{i,j} \leq B,$$

$$\forall (i,j) \in \delta(k_1,k_2) \, \forall k_1,k_2 \in \{1,2,\ldots,k\} \, s.t \, k_1 < k_2 \tag{2.14}$$

$$x_{k_1,k_2}^{i,j} + x_{k_1,k_3}^{i,l} + x_{k_2,k_3}^{j,l} \leq 2, \forall (i,j) \in \delta(k_1,k_2)$$

$$k_1,k_2,k_3 \in \{1,2,\ldots,k\} s.t. \, k_1 < k_2 < k_3 \tag{2.15}$$

$$x_{k_1,k_2}^{i,j} \in \{0,1\}, \forall (i,j) \in \delta(k_1,k_2),$$
$$\forall k_1,k_2 \in \{1,2,\ldots,k\} s.t. \, k_1 < k_2, \tag{2.16}$$

where (2.13) represents the linear objective function, which aims to maximize the total weight of the chosen subgraph. $\delta(k_1, k_2)$ denotes the edge-set between camera k_1 and k_2. (2.14)–(2.16) are the constraints we have to satisfy. $x_{k_1,k_2}^{i,j}$ denotes the edge between ith person in camera

k_1 and j th person in camera k_2. $x_{k_1,k_2}^{i,j}$'s are defined over all possible values of i, j, k_1, and k_2, as described above and together all possible $x_{k_1,k_2}^{i,j}$'s form the decision variable set. $w_{k_1,k_2}^{i,j}$'s are the weights of the corresponding edges and B is our labeling budget. The first constraint (2.14) dictates that we can select at most B number of edges. (2.15) constrain that the subgraph formed by the selected edges be triangle free. (2.16) denotes that optimization variable be binary, where a 1 would indicate that an edge is chosen for manual labeling and 0 otherwise.

Polynomial Time Approximation Optimal Algorithms.   On smaller datasets, we can easily solve our optimization problem using traditional integer programing algorithms, such as cutting plane methods [Marchand et al., 2002], Branch and Cut [Mitchell, 2002], etc. These methods always provide globally optimal solutions. However, as they are exponential time algorithms, we cannot employ them for larger datasets. In order to tackle this challenge, we propose two polynomial time algorithms which drastically improve scalability.

Algorithm 1. This algorithm is motivated by the observation that if we make any cut on the vertex set of a graph, the set of cut crossing edges induces a triangle free subgraph. So if we can make a cut which maximizes the total weight of edges crossing the cut, then we may construct a approximately-optimal solution using those edges. In graph theory, the max-cut problem is well studied where the objective is to find such max-weight cut. As max-cut is also an NP-hard [Michael and David, 1979] problem, there is no known efficient algorithm for it. However there exists a deterministic $1/2$-approximation algorithm for max-cut [Gonzalez, 2007, Mitzenmacher and Upfal, 2017]. Our first algorithm uses this $1/2$-max cut to achieve $1/2$ approximation for our problem. After initialization steps, Max-Cut Select algorithm constructs the subgraph G' using the top B heaviest edges in E. Then it employs the deterministic $1/2$-max cut algorithm on G' to generate a cut $(S, V \setminus S)$. Finally, the algorithm selects the set T of edges which crosses the cut $(S, V \setminus S)$ and returns it.

Algorithm 2. Often in practice, simple greedy heuristics give better performance as compared to other theoretically superior algorithms. This perspective has motivated us to explore greedy strategies for our problem resulting the "Greedy-Select" algorithm. Greedy-Select begins with an empty set T and iterates over the edges in decreasing weight order. In each iteration the algorithm adds the current edge to the set T if the current edge does not form any triangle with the existing edges in T. The algorithm terminates either when we have collected B number of edges in set T or we have iterated over all the edges in the graph.

2.2.2   EXAMPLE RESULTS ON OPTIMAL LABELING SET

Dataset and Settings. We experiment on Market1501 dataset [Zheng et al., 2015a], which is one of the largest person re-identification datasets available today. It has 32,668 images of 1501 persons taken from 6 cameras (see Fig. 2.7 for few sample images). We use the train-test split given in the dataset. Apart from large variations in pose and illuminations, the size of the

Figure 2.7: Six image pairs from the Market1501 dataset. Columns correspond to different persons, rows to different cameras. Best viewed in color.

dataset itself introduces a new level of computational challenge. For Market1501 dataset, the optimization problem we consider, has more than 4.3 millions variables. We use KISS metric learning method [Köstinger et al., 2012] for our experiments. To represent each person node in the graph we use 29600 dimensional LOMO features [Lisanti et al., 2015]. For metric learning, we project the features into 100-dimensional space using PCA. We use euclidean metric as our distance function. In any on-line setting, similarity scores at any time instant can be computed using the learned metric from the previous instance. Given a budget of B, we use a portion of the budget $pB(0 < p < 1)$ [we used $p = 0.7$ for experiments] to select triangle free edges using our optimization problem. However, in cases where the selected edges in a triangle are both negative matches, we cannot infer about the label of the third edge and we may want to gather information about it. For this reason, after first stage of triangle free selection, we employ a greedy top selection mechanism to exhaust the rest of the budget. We use CMC to demonstrate recognition performance at a given budget. We also provide labeling effort vs. recognition performance plots trade-off between the two.

Baselines. In this work, we use top-B edge selection as the baseline strategy. For all our experiments we compare our method against this baseline.

Results. Figure 2.8a demonstrates re-id performance with 8% labels. From Fig. 2.8a, we observe that both of our approaches achieve full set accuracy with this amount of labeling. While

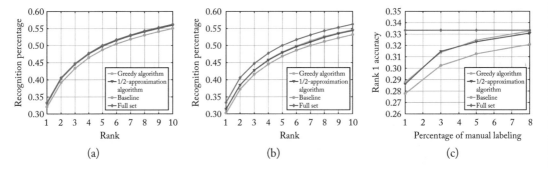

Figure 2.8: Comparison of the proposed approach with baselines on the Market1501 dataset. (a) and (b) are CMC curves with 8% and 3% manual labeling, respectively. (c) presents the plot for manual labeling effort vs. Rank-1 accuracy. Best viewed in color.

with 3% labels, performance of the proposed approaches slightly degrades (see Fig. 2.8b). In Fig. 2.8c, we provide the manual labeling percentage vs. rank-1 accuracy graph. From all these three graphs, it can be easily observed that our approach performs better than the baseline across all the conducted experiments on Market dataset [Roy et al., 2018].

2.3   CONCLUSION

In this chapter, we demonstrated how global camera network constraints in form of consistency can be utilized for improving the accuracy of re-id models and selecting a minimal subset of image pairs for labeling without compromising accuracy. We described novel optimization frameworks and developed efficient algorithms for solving them, with the potential to scale to large camera networks. Analysis of the results indicates robustness of the methods, as well as significant improvements in accuracy over the compared methods. Both of the problems show how supervised re-id performance can be optimized in terms of accuracy and annotation effort, which ultimately need to be considered jointly.

CHAPTER 3

Towards Unsupervised Person Re-identification

While the previous chapter focused on the problem of optimally selecting what to label, we now move to the problem of learning person re-identification models with very limited annotation. We specifically focus on video-based re-id, since the temporal structure in the data can be taken advantage of to compensate for the reduction in supervision, and because it is often practical for applications where video is the default sensing mode.

In recent years, video-based person re-identification has attracted increasing attention because of the above reasons. Some video-based person re-id methods have been proposed and achieved impressive results [Chen et al., 2019b, Li et al., 2020a, Rao et al., 2019, Wang et al., 2020b, Wu et al., 2020, Ye et al., 2020a,b, Ye and Yuen, 2020]. However, this improved performance has predominantly been achieved through *supervised learning*, facilitated by the availability of large amounts of annotated data. However, acquiring identity labels for a large set of unlabeled video tracklets is an extremely time-consuming and cumbersome task. Consequently, methods which can ameliorate this annotation problem and work with limited supervision, such as *unsupervised learning* or *semi-supervised learning* techniques, are of primary importance in the context of person re-id.

In this chapter, we focus on two methods that hold the potential for developing highly scalable person re-identification systems with limited supervision. In the first, we focus on one-shot video person re-id, where the objective is to utilize a small labeled set (only one tracklet per identity) along with a larger unlabeled set of tracklets to obtain a re-id model [Raychaudhuri and Roy-Chowdhury, 2020]. In the second, we aim to develop a fully unsupervised solution for video person re-id by exploiting global network characterstics that does not require any identity labels [Wang et al., 2021b]. Together, they demonstrate the ability to scale person re-identification approaches beyond fully supervised ones, building upon recent successes in unsupervised and self-supervised learning areas.

3.1 TEMPORAL COHERENCE FOR SELF-SUPERVISED, ONE-SHOT VIDEO RE-IDENTIFICATION

We first focus on the semi-supervised task in video person re-ID, specifically, the *one-shot* setting, where only one tracklet per identity is labeled and the objective is to utilize this small labeled set along with a larger unlabeled set of tracklets to obtain a re-id model. The key challenge involved with the one-shot task is figuring out the inter-relationships which exist among the labeled and unlabeled instances. Recent works by Wu et al. [2019b, 2018a] make use of a progressive sampling strategy, where a subset of the pseudo-labeled samples are selected with the size of the subset expanding with each iteration. This prevents an influx of noisy pseudo-labels and, thus, averts the situation of confirmation bias [Arazo et al., 2019]. However, in an effort to control the number of noisy pseudo-labels, most of these methods discard a significant portion of the unlabeled set at each learning iteration. Therefore, the information in the unlabeled set is not maximally utilized for training the model. Due to this inefficient usage of the unlabeled set and the limited number of labeled instances, propagating beliefs directly from the labeled to the unlabeled set is insufficient to fully capture the relationships which exist amongst instances of the unlabeled set.

To resolve the issue of inefficient usage of the unlabeled data, we draw inspiration from the field of self-supervised visual representation learning [Kolesnikov et al., 2019] and propose using *temporal coherence* [Misra et al., 2016, Mobahi et al., 2009, Paul et al., 2018] as a form of self-supervision to maximally utilize the unlabeled data and learn discriminative person specific representations. Temporal coherence is motivated by the fact that features corresponding to a person in a tracklet should be focused on the discriminative aspects related to the person, such as clothing and gait, and ignore background nuances such as illumination and occlusion. This naturally suggests that features should be temporally consistent across the entire duration of the tracklet as the person in a tracklet remains constant.

Based on this intuition, we describe a new framework, *Temporally Consistent Progressive Learning*, which unifies this notion of temporal coherence with a progressive pseudo-labeling strategy. We propose two novel losses to learn such temporally consistent features: *Intra-sequence temporal consistency loss* and the *Inter-sequence temporal consistency loss*. While the first loss employs a local level of consistency by operating on a specific tracklet, the second loss builds on this idea and and extends it by applying temporal consistency both *within and across* tracklets. Using such self-supervised losses, our framework can use the unlabeled data at each iteration of learning, allowing maximal information to be extracted out of it. Additionally, by exploiting two levels of consistency, out approach can better model the relationships amongst the unlabeled instances without being limited by the number of labeled instances.

3.1.1   FRAMEWORK FOR ONE-SHOT VIDEO RE-IDENTIFICATION

Consider that we have a training set of m tracklets, $\mathcal{D} = \{\mathcal{X}_i\}_{i=1}^m$, which are acquired from a camera network. One-shot re-ID assumes that there exists a set $\mathcal{D}_l \subset \mathcal{D}$, which contains a singular labeled tracklet for each identity. Thus, $\mathcal{D}_l = \{(\mathcal{X}_i, y_i)\}_{i=1}^{m_l}$, where $y_i \in \{0, 1\}^{m_l}$ such that y_i is 1 only at dimension i and 0 otherwise, and m_l denotes the number of distinct identities. The rest of the tracklets, $\mathcal{D}_u = \mathcal{D} - \mathcal{D}_l = \{\mathcal{X}_i\}_{i=1}^{m_u}$, do not possess annotations. Our goal is to learn a discriminative person re-ID model $f_\theta(\cdot)$ utilizing both $\mathcal{D}_l$ and $\mathcal{D}_u$. During inference,

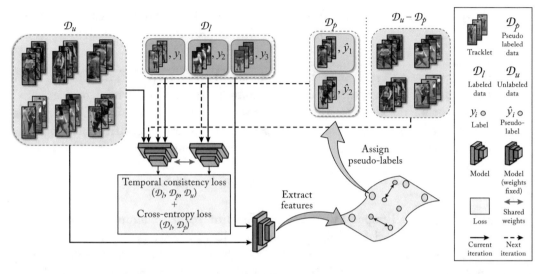

Figure 3.1: A schematic illustration of the proposed framework. Our method makes use of both labeled and unlabeled tracklets at every iteration of model training. The first step involves learning the parameters of the deep model by using temporal consistency as self-supervision and, additionally, softmax loss on the minimal set of annotated tracklets. Next, this model is used to predict pseudo-labels on a few confident samples. These two steps alternate, one after the other, until the entire unlabeled set has been incorporated in terms of pseudo-labels.

$f_\theta(\cdot)$ is used to embed both the probe $\mathcal{X}^q$ and gallery tracklets $\{\mathcal{X}_i^g\}_{i=1}^{m_g}$ into a common space and then rank all the gallery tracklets by evaluating their degree of correspondence to the probe via some metric. What makes this challenging, even more so than the semi-supervised task, is the fact that $m_l \ll m_u$ and each identity has only a single labeled tracklet.

Temporal Coherence as Self-Supervision. We propose to use temporal coherence as a form of self-supervision where consistency across the frames in a tracklet encourages the model to focus on the *local* distribution of the data and learn features which incorporate the specific attributes of the individual in the tracklet by ignoring spurious artifacts such as background and lighting variation. We present two novel losses: Intra-sequence temporal consistency and Inter-sequence temporal consistency, which implement this notion of temporal consistency and show how to integrate them into a self-learning framework toward solving one-shot video re-id task.

Intra-Sequence Temporal Consistency. Given a tracklet $\mathcal{X}$ consisting of frames $\{x_1, \ldots, x_n\}$, intra-sequence consistency involves creating two mini-tracklets $\mathcal{X}^a$ and $\mathcal{X}^p$ by sampling two mutually exclusive sets of frames from $\mathcal{X}$. This is done by the function $\Phi_T(\mathcal{X})$, which first divides the $\mathcal{X}$ into a set of mini-tracklets, each of size $\rho \cdot |\mathcal{X}|$ and then samples from it as follows:

$$\mathcal{X}^{a}, \mathcal{X}^{p} = \Phi_{\mathsf{T}}(\mathcal{X}). \tag{3.1}$$

More specifically, $\Phi_{\mathsf{T}}(\mathcal{X})$ samples from the set $\{\mathcal{X}^1, \mathcal{X}^2, \ldots, \mathcal{X}^{1/\rho}\}$ uniformly without replacement. Here, ρ is a hyper-parameter that controls the size of each mini-tracklet with respect to the size of the tracklet $|\mathcal{X}|$. This ensures that $\mathcal{X}^{a} \cap \mathcal{X}^{p} = \emptyset$, and consequently, these tracklets are temporally incoherent. For all our experiments, ρ is set to 0.2. After obtaining these tracklets the loss forces their respective representations to be consistent temporally with one another as follows:

$$\mathcal{L}_{\mathrm{intra}} = \| f_{\theta}(\mathcal{X}^{a}) - f_{\theta}(\mathcal{X}^{p})) \|_2. \tag{3.2}$$

Inter-Sequence Temporal Consistency. The intra-sequence temporal consistency loss focuses solely on the intra-class similarity. To learn a discriminative person re-id model, the learning process also has to account for the global distribution of the data or the inter-class separability. Specifically, given a tracklet $\mathcal{X}$, we sample two temporally incoherent mini-tracklets in the same manner as mentioned in the previous section. Without loss of generality, we treat one as the anchor $\mathcal{X}^{a}$, and the other one as the positive point $\mathcal{X}^{p}$, which contains the same identity, but temporally perturbed. For the negative instance, we obtain it from the batch nearest neighbors of $\mathcal{X}^{a}$. This is done by creating the corresponding ranking list of tracklets in the batch B, excluding $\mathcal{X}$ and sampling a tracklet $\mathcal{X}^{n}$ uniformly within the range of ranks $[r, 2r]$ as follows:

$$\mathcal{X}^{n} = \Psi(\mathcal{N}_{[r,2r]}(\mathcal{X})), \tag{3.3}$$

where $\Psi(\cdot)$ denotes sampling from a set of elements uniformly. $\mathcal{N}_{[r,2r]}(\mathcal{X})$ indicates the nearest neighbors of $\mathcal{X}$ in the batch (up to a total of B neighbors) which are ranked in the range $[r, 2r]$. Using this range of ranks we filter out possible positive samples and the easy negative samples, which are very low in the ranking list and potentially contribute to zero gradient. The value of r is set to 3 and α to 0.3, for all our experiments. Thus, the inter-sequence temporal consistency loss can be formulated as follows:

$$\mathcal{L}_{\mathrm{inter}} = \max \left\{ 0, \| f_{\theta}(\mathcal{X}^{a}) - f_{\theta}(\mathcal{X}^{p}) \|_2 - \| f_{\theta}(\mathcal{X}^{a}) - f_{\theta}(\mathcal{X}^{n}) \|_2 + \alpha \right\}. \tag{3.4}$$

Temporal Consistency Progressive Learning.   Our approach integrates self-supervision with pseudo-labeling to learn the person re-ID model. Training of this framework alternates between two key steps: (1) representation learning and (2) assignment of pseudo-labels.

Representation Learning. In order to learn the weights of the embedding function $f_{\theta}(\cdot)$, we jointly optimize the following loss function:

$$\mathcal{L} = \sum_{(\mathcal{X},y)\in\mathcal{D}_l} \mathcal{L}_l(\mathcal{X}, y) + \sum_{(\mathcal{X},\hat{y})\in\mathcal{D}_p} \mathcal{L}_l(\mathcal{X}, \hat{y}) + \lambda \left(\sum_{\mathcal{X}\in\mathcal{D}} \mathcal{L}_{\mathrm{intra}}(\mathcal{X}) + \sum_{\mathcal{X}\in\mathcal{D}} \mathcal{L}_{\mathrm{inter}}(\mathcal{X}) \right), \tag{3.5}$$

where $\mathcal{L}_l$ is a standard cross-entropy classification loss applied on all labeled and selected pseudo-labeled tracklets in the dataset. The supervised loss $\mathcal{L}_l$ is optimized by appending a classifier $g_W(\cdot)$ on top of the feature extractor $f_\theta(\cdot)$ as follows:

$$\mathcal{Z} = g_W(f_\theta(\mathcal{X})) = W^T f_\theta(\mathcal{X}) + b \qquad (3.6)$$

$$\mathcal{L}_l = -\log\left(\frac{e^{y^T z}}{\sum_j e^{z_j}}\right), \qquad (3.7)$$

where $f_\theta(\mathcal{X}) \in \mathbb{R}^{d\times 1}$, $W \in \mathbb{R}^{d\times m_l}$, and $b \in \mathbb{R}^{m_l\times 1}$. The value of d represents the feature dimension and is equal to 2048 in our experiments. The labeled set and pseudo-labeled set are denoted by $\mathcal{D}_l$ and $\mathcal{D}_p$, respectively, with $\hat{y}$ denoting the pseudo-labels, while $\mathcal{D}$ refers to the entire set of tracklets. Note that $\mathcal{D}_l \subset \mathcal{D}$ and $\mathcal{D}_p \subset \mathcal{D}$, such that $\mathcal{D}_p \cap \mathcal{D}_l = \emptyset$. The hyper-parameter λ is a non-negative scalar that controls the weight of temporal consistency in the joint loss function.

Assignment of Pseudo-labels. We use the nearest neighbor in the embedding space to assign pseudo-labels—each unlabeled tracklet is assigned a pseudo-label by transferring the label of its nearest labeled neighbor in the embedding space. For $\mathcal{X}_j \in \mathcal{D}_u$,

$$i = \arg\min_{\mathcal{X}_k \in \mathcal{D}_l} \|f_\theta(\mathcal{X}_j) - f_\theta(\mathcal{X}_k)\|_2, \qquad (3.8)$$

$$\hat{y}_j = y_i. \qquad (3.9)$$

After assignment of the pseudo-labels, a confidence criterion is used to choose the most reliable predictions to be used in optimizing $\mathcal{L}_l$ for the next step. Instead of a static threshold, a total of n_t samples are selected at step t by choosing the top n_t unlabeled samples with smallest distance to their corresponding labeled nearest neighbour and added to $\mathcal{D}_p$. A smaller value of the distance implies a more confident pseudo-label prediction. The value of n_t is incremented gradually with t, depending on an enlarging factor $p \in (0, 1)$ where, $n_t = n_{t-1} + pn_u$. Thus, the learning process continues for a total of $(\lfloor 1/p \rfloor + 1)$ steps—until the entire unlabeled set has been assigned confident pseudo-labels. The parameter p controls the trade-off between label estimation accuracy and training time—a smaller value of p leads to better label estimation at the cost of higher training time.

3.1.2 EXAMPLE RESULTS FOR ONE-SHOT VIDEO RE-IDENTIFICATION

Datasets and Settings. We evaluate our method on a standard video person re-id benchmark, namely MARS [Zheng et al., 2016a], which is captured by 6 cameras and contains 20,715 video tracklets of 1,261 identities. Figure 3.2 shows an example of sample tracklets from the MARS dataset. The dataset is split into 625 identities for training and 636 identities for testing. We adopt stochastic gradient descent (SGD) with momentum 0.5 and weight decay 0.0005 to optimize the parameters for 70 epochs, with batch size 16 in each iteration. We set $\lambda = 0.8$ and

Figure 3.2: A total of four sample tracklets from the MARS dataset where Each column represents a distinct individual, with the rows denoting two different views of the same person from two different cameras. We can see that across cameras, the tracklets of the same person vary significantly due to changes in illumination, occlusion, etc. Even within a tracklet, the background varies significantly. Best viewed in color.

the learning rate is initialized to 0.1. For each identity, a tracklet is chosen randomly in camera 1. If camera 1 does not record a particular identity, a tracklet in the next available camera is chosen to ensure each identity has one tracklet for model initialization.

Baselines. We compare with existing one-shot re-id methods which can be broadly divided into two classes: (1) DGM [Ye et al., 2017] and Stepwise Metric [Liu et al., 2017] use the entire pseudo-labeled data at each step of learning and in the process incorporate a lot of noisy labels; and (2) EUG [Wu et al., 2018a] and One-Example Progressive Learning [Wu et al., 2019b] employ progressive sampling. We also consider two baselines: Baseline (one-shot), which utilizes only the one-shot labeled data for training, and Baseline (supervised), which assumes all the tracklets in the training set are labeled; these are trained in a supervised manner using only the cross-entropy loss (IDE). We also compare against state-of-the-art unsupervised methods which report results on video re-ID datasets: BUC [Lin et al., 2019a], UTAL [Li et al., 2019b], and DAL [Chen et al., 2018].

Results. The comparison is presented in Table 3.1. We present the results for different instantiations of our framework: one which uses both the losses (Ours -full) and two others corresponding to usage of the losses individually (Ours -$\mathcal{L}_{\text{intra}}$, Ours -$\mathcal{L}_{\text{inter}}$). The temporal consistency losses lead to consistent gains of in both rank-1 accuracy and mAP over both EUG [Wu et al., 2018a] and One-Shot Progressive Learning [Wu et al., 2019b] methods. To summarize, our

Table 3.1: Comparison of our method with state-of-the-art one-shot and unsupervised methods on MARS dataset. Our approach outperforms all compared methods.

Method	Setting	MARS		
		R-1	R-5	mAP
Baseline: upper bound	Supervised	80.8	92.1	67.4
Ours -full	1-shot	**65.2**	**77.5**	**43.6**
Ours - $\mathcal{L}_{intra}$	1-shot	63.3	75.2	42.9
Ours - $\mathcal{L}_{inter}$	1-shot	64.9	77.5	43.1
One-Shot Prog. [Wu et al., 2019b]	1-shot	62.8	75.2	42.6
EUG [Wu et al., 2018a]	1-shot	62.7	72.9	42.5
Stepwise Metric [Liu et al., 2017]	1-shot	41.2	55.6	19.7
DGM+IDE [Ye et al., 2017]	1-shot	36.8	54.0	16.9
Baseline: lower bound	1-shot	36.2	50.2	15.5
BUC [Lin et al., 2019a]	Unsupervised	61.1	75.1	38.0
UTAL [Li et al., 2019b]	Unsupervised	49.9	66.4	35.2
DAL [Chen et al., 2018]	Unsupervised	46.8	63.9	21.4

approach outperforms all the compared methods by learning an embedding which is temporally consistent.

3.2 GLOBAL NETWORK CONSTRAINTS FOR UNSUPERVISED VIDEO RE-IDENTIFICATION

Despite promising results on common benchmarks, most of the existing methods, including the one discussed in the previous section, are not fully unsupervised and still require some label information, such as source domain labeled data (domain adaption-based unsupervised method) [Fu et al., 2019, Zhang et al., 2019a], to train a model, which limits the scalability of prior methods in practical applications. In recent years, some cross-camera matching methods have been proposed for person re-id or object tracking in a camera network and they achieved impressive performance [Chu and Hwang, 2014, Lin et al., 2020, Zhang and Saligrama, 2016]. However, most of these methods only consider the intra-camera and inter-camera matching correlations of samples independently, but ignore the higher-order relationships across the entire camera network. This may lead to contradictory outputs when matching results from different camera pairs are combined. This aspect was discussed in detail in Chapter 2; here we show how the idea can be used to develop an unsupervised framework for video person re-id.

To illustrate this further, consider a camera network containing three cameras and each of them capture 1–2 persons. Assume that the cross-camera positive matching associations between

(C_1^1, C_2^1), (C_2^2, C_3^1) and (C_1^1, C_3^1) can be obtained independently by using some label estimation methods (C_r^i denotes ith person captured in camera r). We can infer that (C_2^1, C_3^1) is also a positive matching pair because they are matched to the same person C_1^1. However, when these matches from different camera pairs are combined, it leads to an infeasible scenario—C_2^1 and C_2^2 are with the same label. It is hard to distinguish which matches are reliable. While our works described in the previous chapter [Chakraborty et al., 2015, Das et al., 2014] introduce global camera network constraints into person re-id task for reducing the unreliable matches by exploring high-order relationships in a camera network, they require a large number of labeled samples to train their models or the complex optimization method. Motivated by this, we ask an important question in this paper: *Can we develop a reliable cross-camera label estimation strategy, in which the matches are with a guarantee of consistency, for improving the performance of unsupervised re-id without requiring any labeled samples?* This is an especially important problem in the context of many person re-id systems involving large number of cameras.

To address such problems, we propose a consistent cross-view matching framework by exploiting global camera network constraints for unsupervised video person re-id. First, the proposed method is fully unsupervised. We propose to use a first neighbor-based clustering strategy [Sarfraz et al., 2019] to discover the intra-camera label relations and then cross-view matching to explore the inter-camera correlations without requiring any labeled samples for model learning. Second, our approach generates cross-view matches with a guarantee of consistency. Specifically, global camera network constraints are introduced into the cross-view matches to obtain the reliable matching pairs, including a definition for the reliability of matches to reduce the false positive ones. Finally, we learn metric models for camera pairs progressively by using an iterative updating framework which iterates between consistent cross-view matching and metric models learning.

3.2.1 UNSUPERVISED VIDEO RE-IDENTIFICATION

We now present our framework for unsupervised video re-id (see Fig. 3.3), setting up the problem notation, followed by an overview of the algorithm. In camera r, we assume that there are N_r samples and denote it as $\mathcal{I}_r = \left\{ I_r^1, I_r^2, \ldots, I_r^{N_r} \right\}$. A pre-trained feature embedding model $f(\cdot)$ is employed to extract features for the training samples $\mathcal{T}_r = \left\{ T_r^1, T_r^2, \ldots, T_r^{N_r} \right\}$ and the extracted features are used as the inputs of our approach.

Intra-Camera Relationships Exploration. In each camera, there is not much appearance variation between the samples with the same identity. So, we propose utilizing the first neighbor of each sample which can be obtained via fast approximate nearest neighbor methods to explore the label relationships among samples and find the groups in each camera. Specifically, given

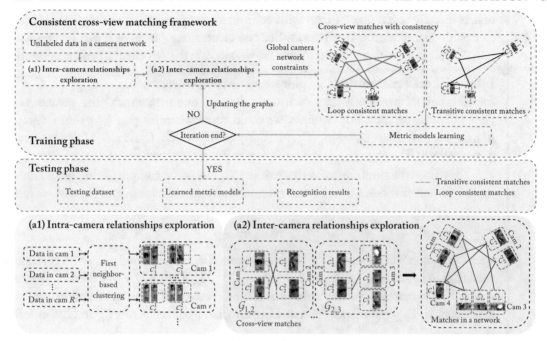

Figure 3.3: Overview of the proposed method. This figure demonstrates the overall framework of the proposed approach. By introducing global camera network constraints into the matches in a camera network, we can select some reliable pairs with a guarantee of consistency. Thereafter, we learn metric models for camera pairs progressively by alternatively mining consistent cross-view matches and updating metric models. (a1) shows the intra-camera clustering for each camera. By using the first neighbor-based clustering algorithm, first neighbor relations can be obtained in each camera. According to Eq. (3.10), the adjacency matrix can be obtained. Thereafter, the connected samples can be clustered together. C_r^i denotes ith cluster in camera r. (a2) illustrates the inter-camera relationships exploration across a camera network. There may be contradictory matches when combining all cross-view matches together, so we introduce global camera network constraints into these matches to obtain reliable pairs. Note that each image in this figure denotes one person tracklet.

the indexes of the first neighbor of each sample in one camera, we define an adjacency matrix:

$$A(i, j) = \begin{cases} 1, & \text{if } i = k_j^1 \text{ or } j = k_i^1 \text{ or } k_i^1 = k_j^1; \\ 0, & \text{otherwise,} \end{cases} \tag{3.10}$$

where k_j^1 denotes that the first neighbor of sample j. The adjacency matrix links each sample i to its first neighbor via $j = k_i^1$, enforces symmetry via $k_j^1 = i$, and links samples $(i; j)$ that have the same neighbor with $k_i^1 = k_j^1$. Equation (3.10) for each camera returns a symmetric sparse matrix directly specifying a graph with connected components as the clusters. It is reasonable to regard each cluster as one person. So, one camera, e.g., camera r, can be denoted as $C_r = \{C_r^1, C_r^2, \ldots, C_r^{n_r}\}$ with n_r clusters/persons, where C_r^i is the ith cluster/person in camera r.

Inter-Camera Relationships Exploration.   We construct a bipartite graph $\mathcal{G} = (U, V, E)$ for each pair of cameras where each node denotes one camera and the vertices are the obtained clusters/persons. For example, we could convert camera pair (p, q) into a graph $\mathcal{G}_{p,q} = (C_p, C_q, E_{M_{p,q}})$, where $C_p = \{C_p^1, C_p^2, \ldots, C_p^{n_p}\}$ and $C_q = \{C_q^1, C_q^2, \ldots, C_q^{n_q}\}$ denote camera p and q, respectively. The edge $E_{M_{p,q}}$ is a matching cost matrix of camera pair (p, q) and each element $e_{M_{p,q}}^{i,j}$ describes the similarity of vertex pair (C_p^i, C_q^j) which is computed through a minimum distance criterion that takes the shortest distance between samples in two clusters, as follows:

$$e_{M_{p,q}}^{i,j} = \min_{T_p^a \in C_p^i, T_q^b \in C_q^j} d_{M_{p,q}}(T_p^a, T_q^b), \tag{3.11}$$

where $M_{p,q}$ denotes a distance metric model learned using estimated pairs with consistency from camera p and q, and $d_{M_{p,q}}(T_p^a, T_q^b) = (T_p^a - T_q^b)^T M_{p,q}(T_p^a - T_q^b)$. We then use the assignment matrix $X_{p,q}$ to represent the matching associations between the vertices across camera pair (p, q), where $x_{p,q}^{i,j}$ in $X_{p,q}$ represents the matching association of the vertex C_p^i and C_q^j, as follows:

$$x_{p,q}^{i,j} = \begin{cases} 1, & \text{if } C_p^i \text{ and } C_q^j \text{ are a matched pair;} \\ 0, & \text{otherwise.} \end{cases} \tag{3.12}$$

In a large camera network, it is common that one camera may not capture every person. In this situation, a person from one camera p can have at most one match from another camera q. In other words, the matching association values in every row or column of the assignment matrix $X_{p,q}$ can all be 0. As a result, the matching association constraints are as follows:

$$\sum_{j=1}^{n_q} x_{p,q}^{i,j} \leq 1, i = 1, 2, \ldots, n_p \text{ and } \sum_{i=1}^{n_p} x_{p,q}^{i,j} \leq 1, j = 1, 2, \ldots, n_q, \tag{3.13}$$

where n_p and n_q are the number of persons/clusters in camera p and camera q, respectively. Finally, to compute the assignment matrix across camera pairs, we formulate it as a binary linear programming with constraints as follows:

$$X_{p,q} = \underset{x_{p,q}^{i,j}}{\arg\min} \sum_{i,j=1}^{n_p,n_q} e_{M_{p,q}}^{i,j} x_{p,q}^{i,j}$$

$$\text{subject to: } x_{p,q}^{i,j} \in \{0, 1\}, \forall i = 1, \ldots, n_p, j = 1, \ldots, n_q$$

$$\sum_{i=1}^{n_p} x_{p,q}^{i,j} \leq 1, \forall j = 1, \ldots, n_q \tag{3.14}$$

$$\sum_{j=1}^{n_q} x_{p,q}^{i,j} \leq 1, \forall i = 1, \ldots, n_p.$$

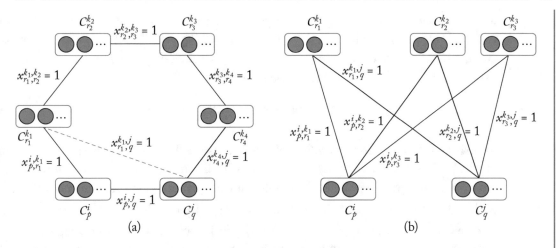

Figure 3.4: An example of consistent cross-view matches in a camera network. (a) demonstrates loop consistent constraint. If $x_{p,q}^{i,j} = 1$ and existing a person k_1 in camera r_1 satisfies $x_{p,r_1}^{i,k_1} x_{r_1,q}^{k_1,j} = 1$, the match (C_p^i, C_q^j) is with consistency. (b) shows a transitive inference consistency pair (C_p^i, C_q^j) and $\mathrm{RT}_{p,q}^{i,j} = 3$.

The assignment matrix set $\mathbf{X} = \{X_{p,q} | p < q\}$ across the pair of cameras in a network can be obtained, where $X_{p,q} = \{x_{p,q}^{i,j} | i = 1, \ldots, n_p, j = 1, \ldots, n_q\}$.

Global Camera Network Constraints. Existing methods, like the Hungarian algorithm [Kuhn, 1955], can be directly used to solve the above binary linear programming problem. However, it is hard to ensure that the obtained matching associations are reliable because the Hungarian algorithm will try to get as many matching associations as possible. Thus, the assignment matrix may contain a lot of false positive matches. In addition, these cross-view matched pairs also do not consider matching consistency in a network of camera. To address this problem, we introduce global camera network constraints including loop consistency constraints and transitive inference consistency constraints into these cross-view matches, which will guarantee the obtained cross-view matching pairs are with consistency.

Loop Consistent Matches. Given two vertices C_p^i and C_q^j from a camera pair (p, q) in a camera network, it can be noted that, for consistency, logical "AND" relationship between the association value $x_{p,q}^{i,j}$ and the set of association values $\{x_{p,r_1}^{i,k_1}, x_{r_1,r_2}^{k_1,k_2}, \ldots, x_{r_n,q}^{k_n,j}\}$ across possible vertices in different cameras has to be maintained, where $r_1, \ldots, r_n, p, q$ denote cameras in a network and $k_1, \ldots, k_n, i, j$ represent the persons captured by corresponding cameras. In other words, the association value $x_{p,q}^{i,j}$ between the two vertices C_p^i and C_q^j has to be 1, and it has to satisfy the indirect matching association $x_{p,r_1}^{i,k_1} x_{r_1,r_2}^{k_1,k_2} \ldots x_{r_4,q}^{k_4,j} = 1$, as shown in Fig. 3.4a. It has been also proven that if the loop consistency constraint is satisfied for every triplet of cameras, it automatically ensures consistency for every possible combination of cameras, taking three or more of them [Das et al., 2014]. Thus, the consistent matching pair $\mathcal{C}_p^i$ and $\mathcal{C}_q^j$ in the network of cameras has to satisfy the direct cross-view matching association $x_{p,q}^{i,j} = 1$ and a person k in camera r should satisfy: $x_{p,r}^{i,k} x_{r,q}^{k,j} = 1$. We formulate it as follows:

$$x_{p,q}^{i,j} = 1 \text{ and } \exists \mathcal{C}_r^k, x_{p,r}^{i,k} x_{r,q}^{k,j} = 1, r \neq p, q. \tag{3.15}$$

Transitive Inference Consistent Matching. We also exploit the transitive relations for enhancing the performance of our cross-view matches. To illustrate the idea, let us consider a plausible scenario, as shown in Fig. 3.4b. Assuming we have positive cross-view matches $(\mathcal{C}_p^i, \mathcal{C}_{r_1}^{k_1})$ and $(\mathcal{C}_{r_1}^{k_1}, \mathcal{C}_q^j)$, then according to the transitive inference we can directly infer that $\mathcal{C}_p^i$ and $\mathcal{C}_q^j$ also have the same label, i.e., $x_{p,r_1}^{i,k_1} x_{r_1,q}^{k_1,j} = 1 \Rightarrow x_{p,q}^{i,j} = 1$. Obviously, by introducing transitive inference, we can increase the number of cross-view matching pairs in a camera network. Usually, in a camera network, with more than two cameras, we define the reliability of the transitive inference-based cross-view matches

$$\text{RT}_{p,q}^{i,j} = \sum_r \sum_{k=1}^{n_r} x_{p,r}^{i,k} x_{r,q}^{k,j}, p \neq q \text{ and } r \neq p, q, \tag{3.16}$$

where p, q and r are cameras in a network. n_r is the number of persons in camera r. $\text{RT}_{p,q}^{i,j}$ denotes the reliability of the pair $(\mathcal{C}_p^i, \mathcal{C}_q^j)$. When the reliability value $\text{RT}_{p,q}^{i,j}$ satisfies $\text{RT}_{p,q}^{i,j} > 1$, we regard the matching pair $(\mathcal{C}_p^i, \mathcal{C}_q^j)$ as a transitive inference consistent match. Note that loop consistency can be regarded as a specific form of the transitive inference consistency constraints. Therefore, combining them together, we define a metric for measuring the reliability of cross-camera matched pairs as follows:

$$\text{RLT}_{p,q}^{i,j} = x_{p,q}^{i,j} + \sum_r \sum_{k=1}^{n_r} x_{p,r}^{i,k} x_{r,q}^{k,j}, r \neq p, q, \tag{3.17}$$

where $\text{RLT}_{p,q}^{i,j}$ represents reliability of cross-view matched pair $(\mathcal{C}_p^i, \mathcal{C}_q^j)$. The larger the value $\text{RT}_{p,q}^{i,j}$ is, the more reliable the transitive inference-based match is, as shown in Fig. 3.4b, i.e., $\text{RT}_{p,q}^{i,j} = 3$. With this score, we obtain the consistent assignment matrices $\hat{X}_{p,q} = \{\hat{x}_{p,q}^{i,j} | i = 1, \ldots, n_p, j = 1, \ldots, n_q\}$ to learn pairwise metric models as

$$\hat{x}_{p,q}^{i,j} = \begin{cases} 1, & \text{if } \text{RLT}_{p,q}^{i,j} > \theta; \\ 0, & \text{otherwise,} \end{cases} \tag{3.18}$$

where θ is a threshold that is used to balance the quality and quantity of the selected matches. Obviously, with the increase in θ value, the selected pairs will be more reliable, however, the number of the matches will be less for training. Thus, we can obtain sufficient and reliable cross-view matches in a camera network by selecting a suitable θ value for the unsupervised video person re-id task.

Metric Learning with Consistent Matches.   Given a consistent assignment matrix $\hat{X}_{p,q}$ for camera pair (p, q), the corresponding metric model $M_{p,q}$ could be learned to update its matching cost matrix $E_{M_{p,q}}$. We use the log-logistic metric learning as the loss function [Liao and Li, 2015b],

$$f_{M_{p,q}}(\mathcal{C}_p^i, \mathcal{C}_q^j) = \log\left(1 + e^{\hat{x}_{p,q}^{i,j}(e_{M_{p,q}}^{i,j} - \mu_{p,q})}\right), \tag{3.19}$$

where $e_{M_{p,q}}^{i,j}$ is the minimum distance between clusters $\mathcal{C}_p^i$ and $\mathcal{C}_q^j$. $\mu_{p,q}$ is the average distance of all consistent matches from camera pair (p, q). Accordingly, for the camera pair (p, q), the overall cost function is

$$F(M_{p,q}; \hat{X}_{p,q}) = \sum_{i=1}^{n_p} \sum_{j=1}^{n_q} w_{i,j} f_{M_{p,q}}(\mathcal{C}_p^i, \mathcal{C}_q^j), M_{p,q} \succeq 0, \tag{3.20}$$

where $w_{i,j}$ is utilized to handle the imbalanced positive and negative pairs, i.e., $w_{i,j} = \frac{1}{N_{pos}}$ if $\hat{x}_{p,q}^{i,j} = 1$, and $\frac{1}{N_{neg}}$ otherwise, and N_{pos} and N_{neg} are the number of consistent matches and negative pairs. During testing, we compute the distance of each query-gallery pair (T_{qu}, T_{ga}) by taking the minimum value under different pair-wise distance metric models. We learn metric models for camera pairs progressively by alternatively mining consistent cross-view matches and updating metric models. In each iteration, the learned metric models are used to update the corresponding matching cost matrix for better exploring inter-camera relationships in a new iteration. Thereafter, the updated consistent cross-view matching correlations could be used to update the previous metric models. Finally, the reliable cross-view matches with consistency and distance metric models can be obtained.

3.2.2   EXAMPLE RESULTS ON UNSUPERVISED VIDEO RE-IDENTIFICATION

Datasets and Settings. We use the standard MARS [Zheng et al., 2016a] video re-id benchmark and adopt both hand-crafted features (LOMO) [Liao et al., 2015b] and deep convolutional neural network (CNN) features for evaluating the performance of our proposed method. We use PCA [Wold et al., 1987] to reduce the dimension to 600. We adopt the pre-trained unsupervised feature embedding model in Lin et al. [2019a] which is designed for unsupervised person re-id to extract the deep CNN features and then ℓ_2 normalize it for experiments. We conduct mean-pooling for each tracklet to get more robust video feature representations.

Baselines. We compare our approach with several state-of-the-art person re-id methods that fall into two main categories: *unsupervised methods* such as GRDL [Kodirov et al., 2016], Un-

Table 3.2: Rank-1, Rank-5, Rank-10 accuracy (%), and mAP (%) comparison with representative unsupervised and semi-supervised approaches on the MARS dataset

Methods	Labels	R1	R5	R10	mAP
GRDL [Kodirov et al., 2016]	None	19.3	33.2	41.6	9.6
UnKISS [Khan and Bremond, 2016]	None	22.3	37.4	47.2	10.6
DGM+LOMO [Ye et al., 2019]	None	24.7	39.4	47.0	11.7
OURS+LOMO	None	**29.2**	**44.3**	**50.5**	**12.2**
OIM [Xiao et al., 2017]	None	33.7	48.1	54.8	13.5
UTM [Riachy et al., 2019]	None	39.7	53.2	–	20.1
DGM+IDE [Ye et al., 2019]	None	48.1	64.7	71.1	29.2
DAL [Chen et al., 2018]	None	49.3	65.9	72.2	23.0
BUC [Lin et al., 2019a]	None	61.1	75.1	80.0	38.0
TAULD [Li et al., 2018a]	None	43.8	59.9	72.8	29.1
UTAL [Li et al., 2019b]	None	49.9	66.4	77.8	35.2
TSSL [Wu et al., 2020]	None	56.3	–	–	30.5
CCE [Lin et al., 2020]	None	62.8	77.2	80.1	**43.6**
OURS	None	**65.3**	**77.8**	**81.3**	41.2
UGA [Wu et al., 2019a]	Intra-camera	59.9	–	–	40.5
Prog. Learning [Wu et al., 2019b]	One-shot	62.8	75.2	80.4	42.6
Stepwise [Liu et al., 2017]	One-shot	41.2	55.5	–	19.6
RACE [Ye et al., 2018]	One-shot	43.2	57.1	62.1	24.5
EUG [Wu et al., 2018b]	One-shot	62.6	74.9	**82.5**	42.4
TCPL [Raychaudhuri and Roy-Chowdhury, 2020]	One-shot	65.2	77.5	–	**43.6**
OURS	None	**65.3**	**77.8**	81.3	41.2

KISS [Khan and Bremond, 2016], DGM+ [Ye et al., 2019] using LOMO feature, DGM+ [Ye et al., 2019] using deep IDE features, OIM [Xiao et al., 2017], DAL [Chen et al., 2018], BUC [Lin et al., 2019a], UTM [Riachy et al., 2019], TAULD [Li et al., 2018a], UTAL [Li et al., 2019b], TSSL [Wu et al., 2020], CCE [Lin et al., 2020], and *semi-supervised methods* such as UGA (intra-camera supervision) [Wu et al., 2019a], Progressive Learning (one-shot setting) [Wu et al., 2019b], Stepwise (one-shot setting) [Liu et al., 2017], RACE (one-shot setting) [Ye et al., 2018], and EUG (one-shot setting) [Wu et al., 2018b]. Note that one-shot assumes a singular labeled tracklet for each identity along with a large pool of unlabeled samples and intra-camera setting works with labels which are provided only for samples within an individual camera view.

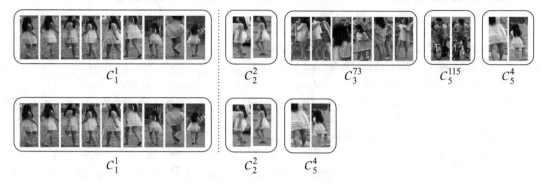

Figure 3.5: Visualization of intra-camera and inter-camera label estimation with/without global network constraints on the MARS dataset. Samples in each box denote the intra-camera clustering results and $\mathcal{C}_r^i$ represents the ith cluster in camera r. The first and second rows show cross-camera matching performance without and with global network constraints, respectively. Note that each image in this figure denotes one person tracklet and we show performance with one person/cluster.

Results. Table 3.2 shows the results. While comparing with unsupervised alternatives, we evaluate our method in two different settings: (1) methods based on handcrafted features: the proposed method significantly outperforms all the compared methods; comparing to DGM+, we achieve 4.5% and 0.5% improvement using the same LOMO feature in rank-1 accuracy and mAP score, respectively; (2) methods based on deep learning: our method also obtains the best recognition performance 65.3% for rank-1 and 41.2% for mAP while comparing to fully unsupervised deep learning-based alternatives, especially, comparing to BUC, the rank-1 accuracy and mAP score are improved by 4.2% and 3.2%, respectively. Compared with the recent CCE [Lin et al., 2020], our method improves the rank-1 accuracy from 62.8–65.3%. As expected, the proposed method performs better while using the deep CNN features compared to the handcrafted LOMO features. We also observe that our method is very competitive while comparing with the semi-supervised methods without requiring any person identity information. Comparing to EUG (one-shot setting), our method achieves 2.7% improvement in rank-1 accuracy.

The visualization of intra-camera and inter-camera label estimation results with/without global network constraints on MARS dataset is shown in Fig. 3.5. It can be seen that the first neighbor-based clustering strategy is effective to group the similar samples in each camera. When introducing global network constraints, the outliers can be removed significantly. Note that we set $\theta = 1$ and iteration $= 0$ to show the results of cross-camera label estimation.

3.3   CONCLUSION

In this chapter, we focused on the problem of video-based person re-identification with very limited supervision. We presented two methods that require minimal to no human annotation to learn scalable models for matching persons in a camera network. While our first approach uses only one-shot labels and self-supervision via temporal coherence, the second method exploits global network constraints for learning a consistent re-id model in an fully unsupervised manner. Both of the approaches demonstrate the importance of using the unlabeled data efficiently and intelligently. For the unsupervised approach, we build upon the global network characteristics that were described in the earlier chapter. Results on standard video re-id benchmark datasets demonstrate the efficacy of the methods over existing alternatives for video person re-identification.

CHAPTER 4

Re-identification in Dynamic Camera Networks

Most of the existing approaches for person re-identification consider a static setting where the number of cameras in the network is fixed. An interesting direction, which has received little attention, is to explore the dynamic nature of a camera network. This could be a mobile network of cameras mounted on robots or an existing network where news cameras are added. In both of these scenarios, the fundamental question comes down to adapting existing re-identification models to newly on-boarded cameras with little additional supervision effort, i.e., learning a transformation between the new camera and the existing ones with limited supervision. Limited supervision is important as, for most applications, there will not be time to collect and label additional data corresponding to the new camera(s).

In this chapter, we focus on the problem of person re-identification in dynamic camera networks and show that it is possible to on-board new camera(s) dynamically to an existing network using transfer learning with limited additional supervision. We ask the question: *Given a camera network where the inter-camera transformations/distance metrics have been learned in an intensive training phase, how can we on-board new cameras into the installed system with minimal additional effort?*. We propose two possible solutions. First, we develop a domain perceptive re-identification framework that can effectively discover and transfer knowledge from the best source camera (already installed) to a newly introduced target camera(s), without requiring a very expensive training phase [Panda et al., 2017a, 2019]. Second, we propose a robust and efficient multiple metric hypothesis transfer learning algorithm to efficiently adapt a new camera to an existing re-identification framework using only source models and limited labeled data, but without using any source camera data from the existing network [Ahmed et al., 2020]. Both of the approaches can greatly increase the flexibility and reduce the deployment cost of new cameras or deal with mobile cameras in many real-world dynamic camera networks.

4.1 ON-BOARDING NEW CAMERAS: TRANSFERRING FROM THE BEST SOURCE CAMERA

We first present an approach to on-board a new camera to an existing setup by identifying the "best" source camera to transfer the learned models from. To illustrate such a problem, let us consider a scenario with $\mathcal{N}$ cameras for which we have learned the optimal pair-wise distance

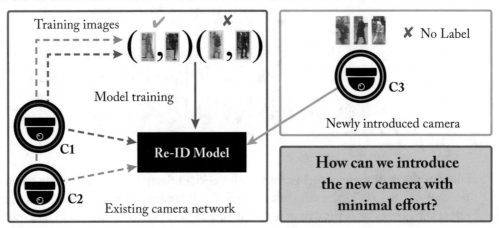

Figure 4.1: Consider an existing network with two cameras C_1 and C_2 where we have learned a re-id model using pair-wise training data from both of the cameras. During the operational phase, a new camera C_3 is introduced to cover a certain area that is not well covered by the existing 2 cameras. Most of the existing methods do not consider such dynamic nature of a re-id model. In contrast, we propose to adapt the existing re-id model in an unsupervised way by exploring: *What is the best source camera to pair with the new camera and how can we exploit the best source camera to improve the matching accuracy across the other camera?*

metrics, so providing high re-id accuracy for all camera pairs. However, during a particular event, a new camera may be temporarily on-boarded to cover a certain related area that is not well-covered by the existing network of $\mathcal{N}$ cameras (see Fig. 4.1 for an illustrative example). Despite the dynamic and open nature of the world, almost all work in person re-identification assume a *static* and *closed* world model of the re-identification problem where the number of cameras are fixed in a network. Given newly introduced camera(s), traditional person re-identification methods will try to relearn the inter-camera transformations/distance metrics using a costly training phase. This is impractical since labeling data in the new camera and then learning transformations with the others is time-consuming, and defeats the entire purpose of temporarily introducing the additional camera. Thus, there is a pressing need to develop *unsupervised* learning models for re-identification that can work in such dynamic camera networks.

Transfer learning/domain adaptation [Daumé III, 2009, Kulis et al., 2011] has been successful in many classical vision problems such as object recognition [Gopalan et al., 2011, Jie et al., 2011, Saenko et al., 2010] and activity classification [Ma et al., 2014, Yang et al., 2013] with multiple classes or domains. The main objective is to scale learned systems from a source domain to a target domain without requiring prohibitive amount of training data in the target domain. Considering a newly introduced camera as target domain, we pose an important question in this paper: *Can unsupervised domain adaptation be leveraged upon for re-identification in a dynamic camera network?* Unlike classical vision problems, e.g., object recognition [Saenko et al., 2010], domain adaptation for re-id has additional challenges. A central issue in domain adaptation is that from *which source to transfer*. When there is only one source of information available which is highly relevant to the task of interest, then domain adaptation is much simpler than in the more general and realistic case where there are multiple sources of information of greatly varying relevance. Re-identification in a dynamic network falls into the latter, more difficult, case. Specifically, given multiple source cameras (already installed) and a target camera (newly introduced), *how can we select the best source camera to pair with the target camera?* The problem can be easily extended to multiple additional cameras being introduced. Moreover, once the best source camera is identified, *how can we exploit this information to improve the re-identification accuracy of other camera pairs?* For instance, let us consider $\mathbf{C}_1$ being the best source camera for the newly introduced camera $\mathbf{C}_3$ in Fig. 4.1. Once the pair-wise distance metric between $\mathbf{C}_1$ and $\mathbf{C}_3$ is obtained, can we exploit this information to improve the re-id accuracy across ($\mathbf{C}_2$–$\mathbf{C}_3$)? This is an especially important problem because it will allow us to now match data in the newly inserted target camera $\mathbf{C}_3$ with all the previously installed cameras.

4.1.1   TRANSFERRING FROM THE BEST SOURCE CAMERA

To adapt re-id models in a dynamic camera network, we first formulate a domain adaptive re-id approach based on geodesic flow kernel which can effectively find the best source camera (out of multiple installed ones) to pair with a newly introduced target camera with minimal additional effort. Then, to exploit information from the best source camera, we propose a transitive inference algorithm that improves the matching performance across other camera pairs in a network [Panda et al., 2017a].

Initial Setup.   Our proposed framework starts with an installed camera network where the discriminative distance metrics between each camera pairs is learned using a off-line intensive training phase. Let there be $\mathcal{N}$ cameras in a network and the number of possible camera pairs is $\binom{\mathcal{N}}{2}$. Let $\{(\mathbf{x}_i^A, \mathbf{x}_i^B)\}_{i=1}^m$ be a set of training samples, where $\mathbf{x}_i^A \in \mathbb{R}^D$ represents feature representation of training a sample from camera view $\mathcal{A}$ and $\mathbf{x}_i^B \in \mathbb{R}^D$ represents feature representation of the same person in a different camera view $\mathcal{B}$. Given the training data, we follow KISS metric learning (KISSME) [Köstinger et al., 2012] and compute the pairwise distance matrices such that distance between images of the same individual is less than distance between images of different individuals. The basic idea of KISSME is to learn the Mahalanobis distance by considering a log likelihood ratio test of two Gaussian distributions. The likelihood ratio test between dissimilar pairs and similar pairs can be written as

$$\mathcal{R}(\mathbf{x}_i^A, \mathbf{x}_j^B) = \log \frac{\frac{1}{c_\mathcal{D}}\exp(-\frac{1}{2}\mathbf{x}_{ij}^T \Sigma_\mathcal{D}^{-1}\mathbf{x}_{ij})}{\frac{1}{c_\mathcal{S}}\exp(-\frac{1}{2}\mathbf{x}_{ij}^T \Sigma_\mathcal{S}^{-1}\mathbf{x}_{ij})}, \tag{4.1}$$

where $\mathbf{x}_{ij} = \mathbf{x}_i^A - \mathbf{x}_j^B$, $\mathcal{C}_D = \sqrt{2\pi|\Sigma_D|}$, $\mathcal{C}_S = \sqrt{2\pi|\Sigma_S|}$, Σ_D and Σ_S are covariance matrices of dissimilar and similar pairs respectively. With simple manipulations, (4.1) can be written as $\mathcal{R}(\mathbf{x}_i^A, \mathbf{x}_j^B) = \mathbf{x}_{ij}^T \mathbf{M} \mathbf{x}_{ij}$, where $\mathbf{M} = \Sigma_S^{-1} - \Sigma_D^{-1}$ is the Mahalanobis distance between covariances associated to a pair of cameras. We follow [Köstinger et al., 2012] and clip the spectrum by an eigen-analysis to ensure $\mathbf{M}$ is positive semi-definite. Note that our approach is agnostic to the choice of metric learning algorithm used to learn the optimal metrics across camera pairs in an already installed network. We adopt KISSME in this work since it is simple to compute and has shown to perform satisfactorily on the person re-id problem.

Discovering the Best Source Camera.   Our approach for discovering the best source camera consists of the following steps: (i) compute geodesic flow kernels between the new (target) camera and other source cameras; (ii) use the kernels to determine distance between them; and (iii) rank source cameras based on distance with respect to the target camera and choose the one with lowest as best source camera.

Let $\{\mathcal{X}^s\}_{s=1}^{N}$ be the N source cameras and $\mathcal{X}^T$ be the newly introduced target camera. To compute the kernels in an unsupervised way, we extend a previous method [Gong et al., 2012] that adapts classifiers in the context of object recognition to the re-identification in a camera network. The main idea of our approach is to compute the low-dimensional subspaces representing data of two cameras (one source and one target) and then map them to two points on a Grassmanian. Intuitively, if these two points are close by on the Grassmanian, then the computed kernel would provide high matching performance on the target camera. In other words, both of the cameras could be similar to each other and their features may be similarly distributed over the corresponding subspaces. For simplicity, let us assume we are interested in computing the kernel matrix $\mathbf{K}^{ST} \in \mathbb{R}^{D \times D}$ between the source camera $\mathcal{X}^S$ and a newly introduced target camera $\mathcal{X}^T$. Let $\check{\mathcal{X}}^S \in \mathbb{R}^{D \times d}$ and $\check{\mathcal{X}}^T \in \mathbb{R}^{D \times d}$ denote the d-dimensional subspaces, computed using Partial Least Squares (PLS) and Principal Component Analysis (PCA) on the source and target camera, respectively. Note that we can not use PLS on the target camera since it is a supervised dimension reduction technique and requires label information for computing the subspaces.

Given both of the subspaces, the closed loop solution to the geodesic flow kernel between the source and target camera is defined as

$$\mathbf{x}_i^{S^T} \mathbf{K}^{ST} \mathbf{x}_j^{T} = \int_0^1 (\psi(\mathbf{y})^T \mathbf{x}_i^S)^T (\psi(\mathbf{y}) \mathbf{x}_j^T) \, d\mathbf{y}, \qquad (4.2)$$

where $\mathbf{x}_i^S$ and $\mathbf{x}_j^T$ represent feature descriptor of ith and jth sample in source and target camera respectively. $\psi(\mathbf{y})$ is the geodesic flow parameterized by a continuous variable $\mathbf{y} \in [0, 1]$ and represents how to smoothly project a sample from the original D-dimensional feature space onto the corresponding low dimensional subspace. The geodesic flow $\psi(\mathbf{y})$ over two cameras can be defined as [Gong et al., 2012],

$$
\psi(\mathbf{y}) = \begin{cases} \tilde{\mathcal{X}}^{\mathcal{S}} & \text{if } \mathbf{y} = 0 \\ \tilde{\mathcal{X}}^{\mathcal{T}} & \text{if } \mathbf{y} = 1 \\ \tilde{\mathcal{X}}^{\mathcal{S}}\mathcal{U}_1 \mathcal{V}_1(\mathbf{y}) - \tilde{\mathcal{X}}_o^{\mathcal{S}}\mathcal{U}_2 \mathcal{V}_2(\mathbf{y}) & \text{otherwise,} \end{cases}
\tag{4.3}
$$

where $\tilde{\mathcal{X}}_o^{\mathcal{S}} \in \mathbb{R}^{D \times (D-d)}$ is the orthogonal matrix to $\tilde{\mathcal{X}}^{\mathcal{S}}$ and $\mathcal{U}_1, \mathcal{V}_1, \mathcal{U}_2, \mathcal{V}_2$ are given by the following pairs of SVDs: $\mathcal{X}^{\mathcal{S}^T}\mathcal{X}^{\mathcal{T}} = \mathcal{U}_1\mathcal{V}_1\mathcal{P}^T$, $\mathcal{X}_o^{\mathcal{S}^T}\mathcal{X}^{\mathcal{T}} = -\mathcal{U}_2\mathcal{V}_2\mathcal{P}^T$. With the above defined matrices, $\mathbf{K}^{\mathcal{ST}}$ can be computed as

$$
\mathbf{K}^{\mathcal{ST}} = \begin{bmatrix} \tilde{\mathcal{X}}^{\mathcal{S}}\mathcal{U}_1 & \tilde{\mathcal{X}}_o^{\mathcal{S}}\mathcal{U}_2 \end{bmatrix} \mathcal{G} \begin{bmatrix} \mathcal{U}_1^T \mathcal{X}^{\mathcal{S}^T} \\ \mathcal{U}_2^T \mathcal{X}_o^{\mathcal{S}^T}, \end{bmatrix}
\tag{4.4}
$$

where $\mathcal{G} = \begin{bmatrix} \mathrm{diag}[1 + \frac{\sin(2\theta_i)}{2\theta_i}] & \mathrm{diag}[\frac{(\cos(2\theta_i)-1)}{2\theta_i}] \\ \mathrm{diag}[\frac{(\cos(2\theta_i)-1)}{2\theta_i}] & \mathrm{diag}[1 - \frac{\sin(2\theta_i)}{2\theta_i}] \end{bmatrix}$ and $[\theta_i]_{i=1}^d$ represents the principal angles between source and target camera. Once we compute all pairwise geodesic flow kernels between a target camera and source cameras using (4.4), our next objective is to find the distance across all those pairs. A source camera which is closest to the newly introduced camera is more likely to adapt better than others. We follow Phillips and Venkatasubramanian [2011] to compute distance between a target camera and a source camera pair. Specifically, given a kernel matrix $\mathbf{K}^{\mathcal{ST}}$, the distance between data points of a source and target camera is defined as

$$
\mathbf{D}^{\mathcal{ST}}(\mathbf{x}_i^{\mathcal{S}}, \mathbf{x}_j^{\mathcal{T}}) = \mathbf{x}_i^{\mathcal{S}^T}\mathbf{K}^{\mathcal{ST}}\mathbf{x}_i^{\mathcal{S}} + \mathbf{x}_j^{\mathcal{T}^T}\mathbf{K}^{\mathcal{ST}}\mathbf{x}_j^{\mathcal{T}} - 2\mathbf{x}_i^{\mathcal{S}^T}\mathbf{K}^{\mathcal{ST}}\mathbf{x}_j^{\mathcal{T}},
\tag{4.5}
$$

where $\mathbf{D}^{\mathcal{ST}}$ represents the kernel distance matrix defined over a source and target camera. We compute the average of a distance matrix $\mathbf{D}^{\mathcal{ST}}$ and consider it as the distance between two camera pairs. Finally, we chose the one that has the lowest distance as the best source camera to pair with the target camera.

Transitive Inference for Re-identification. Once the best source camera is identified, another question that remains in adapting models is: *Can we exploit the best source camera information to improve the re-identification accuracy of other camera pairs?* Let $\{\mathbf{M}^{ij}\}_{i,j=1,i<j}^{\mathcal{N}}$ be the optimal pair-wise metrics learned in a network of $\mathcal{N}$ cameras and $\mathcal{S}^{\star}$ be the best source camera for a newly introduced target camera $\mathcal{T}$. Motivated by the effectiveness of the Schur product in operations research [Kou et al., 2014], we develop a simple yet effective transitive algorithm for exploiting information from the best source camera. The Schur product (a.k.a. Hadamard product) has been an important tool for improving the matrix consistency and reliability in multi-criteria decision making. Our problem naturally fits to such decision making systems since our goal is to establish a path between two cameras via the best source camera. Given the best source camera $\mathcal{S}^{\star}$, we compute the kernel matrix between remaining source cameras and the

target camera as follows:

$$\tilde{\mathbf{K}}^{\mathcal{S}\mathcal{T}} = \mathbf{M}^{\mathcal{S}\mathcal{S}^{\star}} \odot \mathbf{K}^{\mathcal{S}^{\star}\mathcal{T}}, \ \forall [\mathcal{S}]_{i=1}^{\mathcal{N}}, \ \mathcal{S} \neq \mathcal{S}^{\star}, \qquad (4.6)$$

where $\tilde{\mathbf{K}}^{\mathcal{S}\mathcal{T}}$ represents the updated kernel matrix between source camera $\mathcal{S}$ and target camera $\mathcal{T}$ by exploiting information from best source camera $\mathcal{S}^{\star}$. The operator $\odot$ denotes the Schur product of two matrices. Equation (4.6) establishes an indirect path between camera pair $(\mathcal{S},\mathcal{T})$ by marginalization over the domain of possible appearances in best source camera $\mathcal{S}^{\star}$. In other words, camera $\mathcal{S}^{\star}$ plays a role of connector between the target camera $\mathcal{T}$ and all other source cameras.

Summarizing, to adapt re-id models in a dynamic network, we use the kernel matrix $\mathbf{K}^{\mathcal{S}^{\star}\mathcal{T}}$ computed using (4.4) to obtain the re-id accuracy across the newly inserted target camera and best source camera, whereas we use the updated kernel matrices, computed using (4.6), to find the matching accuracy across the target camera and remaining source cameras. Note that although our framework is designed for unsupervised adaptation of re-id models, it can be easily extended if labeled data from the newly introduced camera become available. Specifically, the label information from target camera can be encoded while computing subspaces. That is, instead of using PCA for estimating the subspaces, we can use Partial Least Squares (PLS) to compute the discriminative subspaces on the target data by exploiting the labeled information. PLS has shown to be effective in finding discriminative subspaces by projecting data with labeled information to a common subspace [Geladi and Kowalski, 1986, Schwartz et al., 2009]. This essentially leads to semi-supervised adaptation of re-id models in a dynamic camera network.

4.1.2   EXAMPLE RESULTS ON CAMERA ON-BOARDING

Datasets and Settings. We conduct experiments on RAiD dataset [Das et al., 2014] to verify the effectiveness of our framework. It was collected with a view to have large illumination variation that is not present in most of the publicly available benchmark datasets. In the original dataset 43 subjects were asked to walk through 4 cameras of which 2 are outdoor and 2 are indoor to make sure there is enough variation of appearance between cameras (see Fig. 4.2 for few sample images). The feature extraction stage consists of extracting Local Maximal Occurrence (LOMO) feature proposed in Lisanti et al. [2015] for person representation. The descriptor has 26,960 dimensions. We follow Köstinger et al. [2012] and Paisitkriangkrai et al. [2015b] and apply principle component analysis to reduce the dimensionality to 100 in all our experiments. To compute distance between cameras, as well as re-identification matching score, we use kernel distance [Phillips and Venkatasubramanian, 2011] (Eq. (4.5)) for a given projection metric. We show results using Cumulative Matching Characteristic (CMC) curves and normalized Area Under Curve (nAUC) values, as is common practice in re-id literature [Das et al., 2014, Karanam et al., 2015, Kodirov et al., 2016, Martinel et al., 2016, Zhao et al., 2013]. All the images for each dataset are normalized to 128×64 for being consistent with the evaluations carried out by state-of-the-art methods [Bazzani et al., 2013a, Cheng et al., 2011, Das et al.,

Figure 4.2: A total of six sample image pairs from the RAiD, dataset used for experiments. Columns correspond to different persons, rows to different cameras.

2014]. The train and test set are kept disjoint by picking half of the available data for training set and rest of the half for testing. We repeated each task 10 times by randomly picking 5 images from each identity both for train and test time. The subspace dimension for all the possible combinations are kept 50.

Baselines. We compare with several unsupervised alternatives which fall into two categories: (i) hand-crafted feature-based methods including CPS [Cheng et al., 2011] and SDALF [Bazzani et al., 2013a] and (ii) two domain adaptation-based methods (Best-GFK and Direct-GFK) based on geodesic flow kernel [Gong et al., 2012]. For Best-GFK baseline, we compute the re-id performance of a camera pair by applying the kernel matrix, $\mathbf{K}^{S^\star \mathcal{T}}$ computed between best source and target camera [Gong et al., 2012], whereas in Direct-GFK baseline, we use the kernel matrix computed directly across source and target camera using (4.4). The purpose of comparing with Best-GFK is to show that the kernel matrix computed across the best source and target camera does not produce optimal re-id performance in computing matching performance across other source cameras and the target camera. On the other hand, the purpose of comparing with Direct-GFK baseline is to explicitly show the effectiveness of our transitive algorithm in improving performance in a dynamic network.

Results. Figure 4.3 shows results for all possible camera combinations on RAiD dataset. The following observations can be made from Fig. 4.3: (i) the proposed framework for re-identification

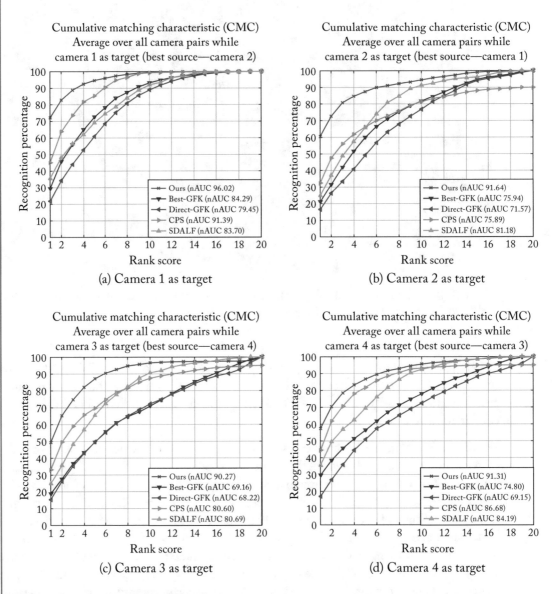

Figure 4.3: CMC curves for RAiD dataset with four cameras. Plots (a, b, c, d) show the performance of different methods while introducing camera 1, 2, 3, and 4, respectively, to a dynamic network. Our method significantly outperforms all the compared baselines for each case of the dynamic network. Best viewed in color.

consistently outperforms all compared unsupervised methods on all three datasets by a significant margin. (ii) among the alternatives, CPS baseline is the most competitive. However, the gap is still significant due to the two introduced components working in concert: discovering the best source camera and exploiting its information for re-identification. The rank-1 performance improvements over CPS is 24.50% on RAiD dataset. (iii) Best-GFK works better than Direct-GFK in most cases, which suggests that kernel computed across the best source camera and target camera can be applied to find the matching accuracy across other camera pairs in re-identification. (iv) Finally, the performance gap between our method and Best-GFK (maximum improvement of 17% in nAUC on RAiD) shows that the proposed transitive algorithm is effective in exploiting information from the best source camera while computing re-id accuracy across camera pairs.

Figure 4.4 shows the effectiveness of our transitive algorithm in person re-identification on RAiD dataset. As can be seen from the figures, the proposed framework (Ours) perform best in matching persons (within rank-2) across camera pairs by exploiting information from the best source camera.

4.2   ON-BOARDING NEW CAMERAS *WITHOUT* ACCESS TO SOURCE CAMERA DATA

The work described above addresses the problem of on-boarding new cameras to a network by utilizing old data that were collected in the original camera network, combined with newly collected data in the expanded network and source metrics to learn new pairwise metrics. It assumes the same set of people in all camera views, including the new camera (i.e., before and after on-boarding new cameras) for measuring the view similarity. However, this is unrealistic in many surveillance scenarios as source camera data may have been lost or not accessible due to privacy concerns. Additionally, new people may appear after the target camera is installed who may or may not have appeared in existing cameras.

Motivated by this observation, we pose an important question: *How can we swiftly on-board new camera(s) in an existing re-id framework (i) without having access to the source camera data that the original network was trained on, and (ii) relying upon only a small amount of labeled data during the transient phase, i.e., after adding the new camera(s). (see Fig. 4.5 for an illustrative example).* Unlike the previous approach, knowledge transfer in this setting is challenging, because of limited labeled data and absence of source camera data while on-boarding new cameras. To solve these problems, we develop an efficient model adaptation approach using *hypothesis transfer learning* that aims to transfer the knowledge using only source models (i.e., learned metrics) and limited labeled data, but without using any original source camera data. *Only a few labeled identities that are seen by the target camera, and one or more of the source cameras, are needed for effective transfer of source knowledge to the newly introduced target cameras.* Specifically, given a set of pairwise source metrics and limited labeled target data after adding the new camera(s), we develop an efficient convex optimization formulation based on hypothesis transfer learning [Du et al.,

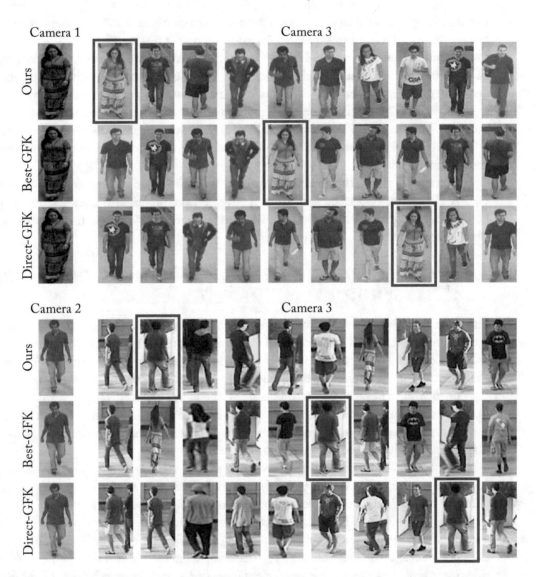

Figure 4.4: Visual comparison of two random persons from a newly introduced camera to top 10 matches from an already introduced camera in RAiD dataset. Top row: our matching result across camera pairs using the transitive algorithm. Middle row: matching the same person using Best-GFK. Bottom row: matching the same person using Direct-GFK. Best viewed in color.

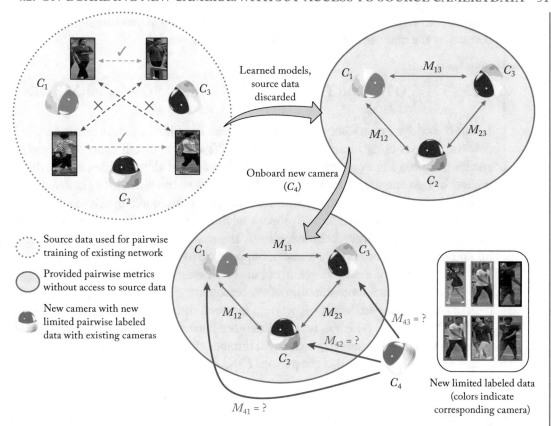

Figure 4.5: Consider a three-camera (C_1, C_2, and C_3) network, where we have only three pairwise distance metrics (M_{12}, M_{23}, and M_{13}) available for matching persons, and no access to the labeled data due to privacy concerns. A new camera, C_4, needs to be added into the system quickly, thus, allowing us to have only very limited labeled data across the new camera and the existing ones. Our goal in this book is to learn the pairwise distance metrics (M_{41}, M_{42}, and M_{43}) between the newly inserted camera(s) and the existing cameras, using the learned source metrics from the existing network and a small amount of labeled data available after installing the new camera(s).

2017, Kuzborskij and Orabona, 2013] that minimizes the effect of negative transfer from any outlier source metric while transferring knowledge from source to the target cameras. We learn the weights of different source metrics and the optimal matching metric jointly by alternating minimization, where the weighted source metric is used as a biased regularizer that aids in learning the optimal target metric only using limited labeled data. The proposed method, essentially, learns which camera pairs in the existing source network best describe the environment that is covered by the new camera and one of the existing cameras.

4.2.1 HYPOTHESIS TRANSFER LEARNING FOR ON-BOARDING NEW CAMERAS

Let us consider a camera network with K cameras for which we have learned a total $N = \binom{K}{2}$ pairwise metrics using extensive labeled data. We wish to install some new camera(s) in the system that need to be operational soon after they are added, i.e., without collecting and labeling lots of new training data. We do not have access to the old source camera data, rather, we only have the pairwise source distance metrics. Using the source metrics and the limited pairwise source-target labeled data, we propose solving a constrained convex optimization problem (4.7) that aims to transfer knowledge from the source metrics to the target efficiently while minimizing the risk of negative transfer. Suppose we have access to the optimal distance metric $M_{ab} \in \mathbb{R}^{d \times d}$ for the a and bth camera pair of an existing re-id network, where d is the dimension of the feature representation of the person images and $a, b \in \{1, 2 \ldots K\}$. We also have limited pairwise labeled data $\{(x_{ij}, y_{ij})\}_{i=1}^{C}$ between the target camera τ and the source camera s, where $x_{ij} = (x_i - x_j)$ is the feature difference between image i in camera τ and image j in camera s, $C = \binom{n_{\tau s}}{2}$, where $n_{\tau s}$ is the total number of ordered pair images across cameras τ and s, and $y_{ij} \in \{-1, 1\}$. $y_{ij} = 1$ if the persons i and j are the same person across the cameras, and -1 otherwise.

Note that our approach does not need the presence of every person seen in the new target camera across all the source cameras; rather, it is enough for some people in the target camera to be seen in at least one of the source cameras, in order to compute the new distance metric across source-target pairs. Let S and D be defined as $S = \{(i, j) \mid y_{ij} = 1\}$ and $D = \{(i, j) \mid y_{ij} = -1\}$. Our main goal is to learn the optimal metric between target and each of the source cameras by using the information from all the pairwise source metrics $\{M_j\}_{j=1}^{N}$ and limited labeled data $\{(x_{ij}, y_{ij})\}_{i=1}^{C}$. In standard metric learning context, the distance between two feature vectors $x_i \in \mathbb{R}^d$ and $x_j \in \mathbb{R}^d$ with respect to a metric $M \in \mathbb{R}^{d \times d}$ is calculated by $\sqrt{(x_i - x_j)^{\top} M (x_i - x_j)}$. Thus, we formulate the following optimization problem for calculating the optimal metric $M_{\tau s}$ between target camera τ and the sth source camera, with n_s and n_d number of similar and dissimilar pairs, as follows:

$$
\begin{aligned}
\underset{M_{\tau s}, \beta}{\text{minimize}} \quad & \frac{1}{n_s} \sum_{(i,j) \in S} x_{ij}^{\top} M_{\tau s} x_{ij} + \lambda \| M_{\tau s} - \sum_{j=1}^{N} \beta_j M_j \|_F^2 \\
\text{subject to} \quad & \frac{1}{n_d} \sum_{(i,j) \in D} (x_{ij}^{\top} M_{\tau s} x_{ij}) - b \geq 0, \ M_{\tau s} \succeq 0, \\
& \beta \geq 0, \ \|\beta\|_2 \leq 1.
\end{aligned}
\tag{4.7}
$$

The above objective consists of two main terms. The first term is the normalized sum of distances of all similar pair of features between camera τ and s with respect to the Mahalanobis metric $M_{\tau s}$, and the second term represents the Frobenius norm of the difference of $M_{\tau s}$ and weighted combination of source metrics squared. λ is a regularization parameter to balance the two terms. Note that the second term in (4.7) is essentially related to hypothesis transfer learning [Du et al., 2017, Kuzborskij and Orabona, 2013] where the hypotheses are the source metrics. The first constraint represents that the normalized sum of distances of all dissimilar pairs of features with respect to $M_{\tau s}$ is greater than a user defined threshold b, and the second constraints the distance metrics to always lie in the positive semi-definite cone. While the third constraint keeps all the elements of the source weight vector non-negative, the last constraint ensures that the weights should not deviate much from zero (through upper-bounding the ℓ-2 norm by 1).

Optimization.   The proposed optimization problem (4.7) is jointly convex over $M_{\tau s}$ and β. To solve this optimization over large size matrices, we devise an iterative algorithm to efficiently solve (4.7) by alternatively solving for two sub-problems. Specifically, in the first step, we fix the weight β and take a gradient step with respect to M in the descent direction with step size α. Then, we project the updated M onto C_1 and C_2 in an alternating fashion until convergence. In the next step, we fix the updated M and take a step with size γ toward the direction of negative gradient with respect to β. In the last step, we simply project β onto the set C_3. Note that our approach minimizes the risk of negative transfer and performs close to fully supervised case even when a small amount of labeled data is available.

4.2.2   EXAMPLE RESULTS ON CAMERA ON-BOARDING WITHOUT SOURCE DATA

Datasets and Settings. We test the effectiveness of our method by experimenting on the same RAiD dataset [Das et al., 2014] which consists of images of 43 persons captured in 4 cameras. We use the Local Maximal Occurrence (LOMO) feature [Lisanti et al., 2015] of length 29,960 for person representation and follow standard PCA technique to reduce the feature dimension to 100, as in Panda et al. [2017a].

Baselines. We compare our approach with the following methods. (1) Two variants of Geodesic Flow Kernel (GFK) [Gong et al., 2012] such as Direct-GFK where the kernel between a source-target camera pair is directly used to evaluate the accuracy and Best-GFK where GFK between the best source camera and the target camera is used to evaluate accuracy between all source-target camera pairs as in the previous approach. (2) State-of-the-art method for on-boarding new cameras [Panda et al., 2017a, 2019] that uses transitive inference over the learned GFK across the best source and target camera (Adapt-GFK). (3) Clustering-based Asymmetric MEtric Learning (CAMEL) method of Yu et al. [2017], which projects features from source and target camera to a shared space using a learned projection matrix. In addition to the above base-

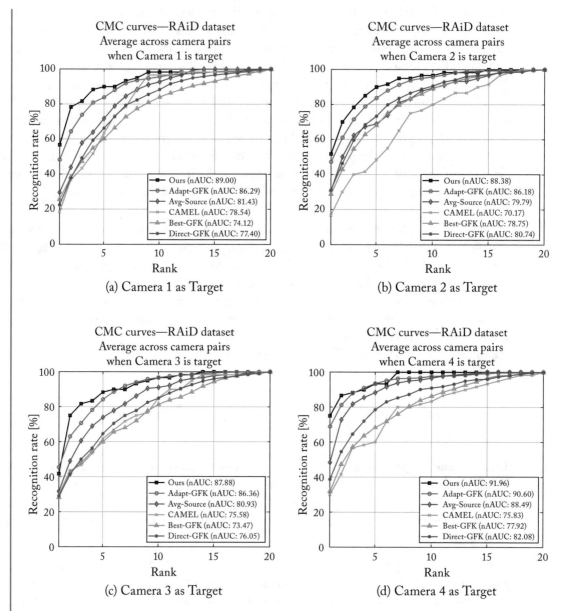

Figure 4.6: CMC curves for RAiD dataset with four cameras. Plots (a, b, c, d) show the performance of different methods while introducing camera 1, 2, 3, and 4, respectively, to a dynamic network with no access to the labeled data due to privacy concerns. Our method significantly outperforms the most competitive Adapt-GFK baseline by a margin of 2.71%, 2.2%, 1.52%, and 1.36% in nAUC for camera 1, 2, 3, and 4 as target, respectively. Best viewed in color.

lines, we compare against the accuracy of average of the source metrics (Avg-Source) by applying it directly over the target test set.

Results. Figure 4.6 shows results for all possible camera combinations on RAiD dataset. In all cases, our method outperforms all the compared methods. The most competitive methods are those of Adapt-GFK and Avg-Source that also use source metrics. For the remaining methods, we see the limitation of only using limited target data to compute the new metrics. We also observe that even without accessing the source training data that was used for training the network before adding a new camera, our method outperforms the GFK-based methods that use all the source data in their computations. To summarize, the experimental results show that our method performs better with limited supervision, as it is able to adapt multiple source metrics through reducing negative transfer by dynamically weighting the source metrics.

4.3   CONCLUSION

In this chapter, we discussed a critically important and challenging person re-identification problem regarding on-boarding one or multiple new cameras into an existing re-identification system with limited additional supervision. We showed adaptation of re-identification models can be addressed effectively using transfer learning with and without access to source data after installing the new camera(s). These methods demonstrate the ability to scale person re-identification with little to no additional supervision and we hope that this will spur future research into person re-identification in mobile networks.

CHAPTER 5

Future Research Directions

In the last few chapters, we have discussed some recent developments in matching persons across a network of non-overlapping cameras. We first demonstrated how global camera network constraints can be utilized for improving both accuracy of models and selecting a minimal subset of image pairs for labeling in supervised person re-identification. We presented polynomial-time algorithms to solve the optimization problems in order to scale up the proposed methodologies for large camera networks. Thereafter, we considered the problem of video person re-identification and showed that how one-shot labels and self-supervision can be used to learn video re-id models with limited supervision. We specifically demonstrated the importance of using unlabeled data, which can be used very effectively to learn scalable re-identification models. Finally, we discussed two very important challenging person re-identification problems regarding on-boarding new cameras that can greatly reduce deployment cost of new cameras in many real-world surveillance applications, and lead to methods to deal with mobile camera networks.

Future research in person re-identification can evolve along many themes. In this section, we discuss several future research directions from five important aspects, including knowledge transfer across networks, learning in mobile networks, human-in-the loop person re-identification, adversarial robust re-identification, and efficient model deployment in resource-limited applications.

5.1 KNOWLEDGE TRANSFER ACROSS NETWORKS

We have shown that it is possible to add a new target camera to an existing network of source cameras using transfer learning with no additional supervision for the new camera. An extension of this problem is on transferring learned models from one network to an entirely new network of cameras, by identifying similarities between the observations in the two networks. This is still a largely under-addressed problem with many challenges. Specifically, how to leverage specific features and knowledge of multiple networks and optimally adapt them to an unlabelled target network remains to be elaborated. Given multiple existing source networks and a newly installed target network with limited labeled data, we first need to find the relevance/similarity of each source network, or parts thereof, in terms of amount of knowledge that it can transfer to a target network. Developing efficient statistical measures for finding relevance in a multi-camera network with significant changes in viewing angle, lighting, background clutter, and occlusion can be a very interesting future work. Attention transfer techniques [Zagoruyko and Komodakis, 2016] along with distillation can be adopted to transfer knowledge from a number of existing labeled networks to an unlabeled target network containing targets which never appeared in the source network. Domain-invariant mapping network [Song et al., 2019] or mutual learning with brainstorming [Zhai et al., 2020] can also be utilized to accommodate the heterogeneity of different source networks/models while transferring knowledge to a unknown target camera/domains. Furthermore, the similarities between the networks should not only be based upon the observed features in the cameras, but also the transitions between them, i.e., if transformations between observations in a pair of cameras in the source domain and target domain are similar, that should be reflected in the process of knowledge transfer. While these existing works show promising performance on standard datasets, knowledge transfer across networks for person re-identification is still an open issue.

5.2   LEARNING IN MOBILE CAMERA NETWORKS

Existing re-identification works including our works discussed in previous chapters are conventionally formulated as a one-to-one set-matching problem between two or more fixed cameras, for which an effective model can be learned. Despite the success of these works in matching persons across static cameras, considering mobile cameras (e.g., network of robots) opens up exciting new research problems in terms of thinking about learning such data association models. Mobile camera networks usually operate in a variety of conditions, with varying lighting, traffic patterns, scene clutter, etc. It is not possible to learn transformation models between every possible pair of views in two mobile cameras due to the constantly changing nature of the videos being captured. Thus, in order to efficiently learn data association models, we need the training data to represent the variety of scenarios that will be encountered by the mobile cameras. Toward this, one can develop a semi-supervised pipeline that uses limited manual training data along with newly generated data through a generative adversarial network (GAN) [Goodfellow et al., 2014]. One initial approach could be to use the unlabeled samples produced by a Multi-view Generative Adversarial Network (Mv-GAN) [Chen and Denoyer, 2017] in conjunction with the labeled training data to learn view-invariant features in a mobile network. Moreover, apart from generating samples, we may need to evolve the learned models over time based on the observed features. In particular, assume that we have a learned a re-identification model at some time, t_0, that is a function of the observed features at that time instant. As the agent moves, we constantly calculate the changes in the features of the observed targets. This can be done in a suitable subspace or manifold that best represents the features such that the change in feature space can be mapped back to the re-identification model space. The propagation of errors needs to be tracked; when the error is unacceptable, the re-identification models can be reinitialized by asking for additional human input, which leads to another, largely unaddressed, problem of person re-identification with a human in-the-loop.

5.3   HUMAN-IN-THE-LOOP RE-IDENTIFICATION

Most traditional multi-camera person re-identification systems may not be suitable for situations when new data arrives continuously or all the data is not available for labeling beforehand. In the presence of a continuous inflow of unlabeled images containing both previously seen and unseen persons, inputs from a human are necessary. A scalable approach to reduce the labeling effort requires a small number of questions (label requests) to be asked without compromising the performance. The human in the loop cannot only provide labels to the incoming images but also improve the learned model by providing most appropriate feedback. The overall effect of such a hybrid strategy is that starting with a few annotated images, the system begins to improve via a symbiotic relationship between the man and the machine. The machine assists the human to speed the annotation and the human assists the machine to update itself with more annotation; this allows for more and more distinct persons to be re-identified as more and more images come in Das et al. [2015]. However, manual labeling of images with feedback is often very expensive and, hence, the effective use of human resource involves limiting the annotation effort which, in the presence of a large amount of data, implies automatically supplying a diverse, but non-redundant, set of examples to the human experts to label.

A human-in-the-loop iterative framework for progressively and judiciously selecting a sparse but informative set of samples, with minimal overlap with previously labeled images was presented in Das et al. [2017]. The overall scheme of the approach is shown in Fig. 5.1. The "Representative Selection" module (shown in the middle of Fig. 5.1) receives unlabeled images of persons from multiple sensors and selects a few informative representatives from them. Next, redundant images inside the samples chosen in this step are removed inside the "intra-iteration redundancy reduction" module. Now the active samples or the representatives filtered by this "intra-iteration redundancy reduction" module are presented to the human annotators seeking for labels. The labeled samples form a dictionary which is fed to the representative selection framework so that in the next iteration those representatives from the unlabeled pool are chosen which are maximally non-redundant with the labeled images in the dictionary. This cycle goes on as new images come from the streaming videos. While the approach in Das et al. [2017] shows the potential of human and computer interaction in person re-identification, we need to develop efficient active learning mechanisms to reduce both the computational complexity as well as the additional manual effort required for human-in-the-loop systems. Developing novel graph-based approaches or subset selection methods, like Wang et al. [2016b] and Martinel et al. [2016] for selecting highly informative samples is an interesting future research problem toward minimizing human labeling effort. Design of hybrid human-in-the-loop systems is very crucial for realizing the potential of person re-identification in practical surveillance applications, but it has received very little attention in the research community.

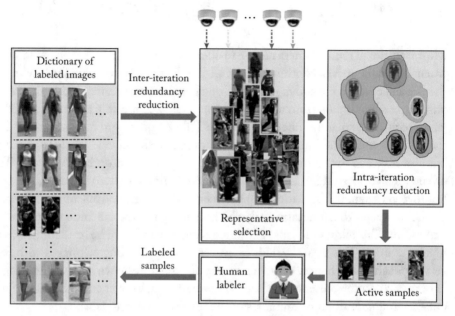

Figure 5.1: A human-in-the-loop system for labeling images in person re-identification. Given incoming streaming videos and detected person images, the framework iteratively chooses small sets of informative images to be labeled by human annotators. These informative images, called the "active samples," are chosen starting with completely unlabeled pool of detections. The human annotators give identities (labels) to the active samples by comparing with a gallery of already labeled samples (denoted here as "Dictionary of labeled images"). Initially, the labeled dictionary is empty and is incrementally built as more and more data becomes available.

5.4   ADVERSARIAL ROBUST RE-IDENTIFICATION

Deep person re-identification systems, similar to other recognition models, inherit the vulnerability of deep neural networks to malicious attacks of visually in-conspicuous adversarial perturbations. Detection of adversarial examples is, therefore, a fundamental requirement for robust re-identification systems because the insecurity of re-id systems may cause severe losses in many critical applications. Person re-identification is defined as a ranking problem rather than a classification problem and thus existing defense methods for image classification [Cohen et al., 2020, Kurakin et al., 2016, Tramèr et al., 2017] do not often fit the person re-identification problem. However, different from the prediction label in classification task, the top-K retrievals output by a person re-id system contain richer information and can be potentially employed to detect adversarial attacks. For example, context inconsistency [Li et al., 2020b] in the retrieval results can be utilized to detect adversarial perturbation attacks on person re-id systems. While these strategies seem simple in practice, they are hard to realize. One needs to make sure that the consistency checks are robust to noise; otherwise, one can expect a large false positive rate (i.e., benign inputs can be misclassified as adversarial) that can significantly hurt the usability of the re-id system. Development of robust person re-identification systems also calls for the study of different white-box and black-box adversarial attacks along with defenses, which have received wide attention in the context of classification-based tasks [Bai et al., 2020]. Investigating physical-world attacks on deep person re-identification systems in multi-camera environments [Wang et al., 2019] is also another interesting research direction that usually faces more complex physical conditions compared to classification-based systems. A recent work by Wang et al. [2021a] presents a multi-expert adversarial attack detection approach to detect adversarial attacks in re-id systems by checking context inconsistency, which is suitable for any deep learning systems. Specifically, three kinds of context inconsistencies caused by adversarial attacks are employed to learn a detector for detecting adversarial attacks, i.e., (a) the embedding distances between a perturbed query person image and its top-K retrievals are generally larger than those between a benign query image and its top-K retrievals, (b) the embedding distances among the top-K retrievals of a perturbed query image are larger than those of a benign query image, and (c) the top-K retrievals of a benign query image obtained with multiple expert re-id models tend to be consistent, which is not preserved when attacks are present.

5.5   EFFICIENT MODEL DEPLOYMENT

Despite impressive results on commonly used benchmark datasets, the accuracy obtained by most of existing person re-identification models usually grows proportionally with their complexity and computational cost. This poses an issue for deploying these models in many resource-limited applications. In particular, this creates a problem for realizing pervasive deep learning, which requires real-time inference, with low energy consumption and high accuracy, in resource-constrained environments. Thus, it is important to design efficient and lightweight models to address scalability issue for practical model deployment. Design of compact architectures or model compression could greatly help in reducing inference complexity of deep re-id models [Cheng et al., 2017, Quan et al., 2019, Tan and Le, 2019]. Adaptively adjusting the model parameters (e.g., width, depth, resolutions) according to the hardware configurations can also provide a solution to adapt re-id models with different computational resources [Wang et al., 2018]. Building efficient networks requires understanding both space and time, and hence, it is often hard to hand-design the right networks that can efficiently capture this information. This will require an automatic neural architecture search [Zoph and Le, 2016] for finding modules that capture different temporal or spatial resolutions to provide complementary representations that benefit re-identification, automatically searching the connection/fusion weights between different representations, and searching optimized networks based on runtime or memory usage. Another interesting direction for efficient model deployment is to adopt dynamic neural networks that are able to strategically allocate computations on demand at test time, by selectively activating model components conditioned on the input [Bengio et al., 2013, Meng et al.,

2020]. This will ensure that less computation is spent on canonical samples that are relatively easy to match, or on less informative spatial/temporal locations of an input. Co-designing re-id models for a particular target platform is also very important as the overhead of deep models (in terms of latency and energy) is hardware dependent. Achieving efficient, real-time inference with optimal accuracy requires rethinking the design, training and testing of re-id models, which has not been addressed to the full extent in the person re-identification literature [Gong et al., 2020, Quan et al., 2019].

5.6   WHAT DOES THE FUTURE HOLD?

Person re-identification is an interesting and active area of research in computer vision and machine learning with a promise for addressing problems in many real-world applications where there is a critical need for such technology, e.g., disaster response, wide area surveillance, forensic applications, etc. While person re-identification in multi-camera networks has been extensively studied in the last few years, several challenging problems, like learning re-identification models with limited supervision, video person re-identification, and person re-identification in dynamic camera networks, are very much in their infancy. The area holds a lot of promise for a number of reasons—basic research problems that span multiple disciplines like computer vision, signal processing, pattern recognition, machine learning, estimation theory, to interdisciplinary research problems that bring together computer science, electrical engineering, mathematics, and statistics, and technology development that will transition the research into specific application domains.

Bibliography

Ahmed, Ejaz, Jones, Michael, and Marks, Tim K. (2015). An improved deep learning architecture for person re-identification. In *CVPR*. DOI: 10.1109/cvpr.2015.7299016 4

Ahmed, Sk Miraj, Lejbolle, Aske R., Panda, Rameswar, and Roy-Chowdhury, Amit K. (2020). Camera on-boarding for person re-identification using hypothesis transfer learning. In *Proc. of the IEEE/CVF Conference on Computer Vision and Pattern Recognition*, pages 12144–12153. DOI: 10.1109/cvpr42600.2020.01216 7, 41

Aich, Abhishek, Zheng, Meng, Karanam, Srikrishna, Chen, Terrence, Roy-Chowdhury, Amit K., and Wu, Ziyan (2021). Spatio-temporal representation factorization for video-based person re-identification. In *Proc. of the IEEE International Conference on Computer Vision*. 4

Aodha, Oisin Mac, Campbell, Neill D. F., Kautz, Jan, and Brostow, Gabriel J. (2014). Hierarchical subquery evaluation for active learning on a graph. In *IEEE Conference on Computer Vision and Pattern Recognition*. DOI: 10.1109/cvpr.2014.79 6

Arazo, Eric, Ortego, Diego, Albert, Paul, O'Connor, Noel E., and McGuinness, Kevin (2019). Pseudo-labeling and confirmation bias in deep semi-supervised learning. DOI: 10.1109/ijcnn48605.2020.9207304 6, 26

Assari, Shayan Modiri, Idrees, Haroon, and Shah, Mubarak (2016). Human re-identification in crowd videos using personal, social and environmental constraints. In *European Conference on Computer Vision*, pages 119–136, Springer. DOI: 10.1007/978-3-319-46475-6_8 7

Avraham, Tamar, Gurvich, Ilya, Lindenbaum, Michael, and Markovitch, Shaul (2012a). Learning implicit transfer for person re-identification. In *ECCV*. DOI: 10.1007/978-3-642-33863-2_38 4

Avraham, Tamar, Gurvich, Ilya, Lindenbaum, Michael, and Markovitch, Shaul (2012b). Learning implicit transfer for person re-identification. In *European Conference on Computer Vision, Workshops and Demonstrations*, pages 381–390. DOI: 10.1007/978-3-642-33863-2_38 14, 15

Bai, Song, Bai, Xiang, and Tian, Qi (2017). Scalable person re-identification on supervised smoothed manifold. *ArXiv Preprint ArXiv:1703.08359*. DOI: 10.1109/cvpr.2017.358 7

Bai, Song, Li, Yingwei, Zhou, Yuyin, Li, Qizhu, and Torr, Philip H. S. (2020). Adversarial metric attack and defense for person re-identification. *IEEE Transactions on Pattern Analysis and Machine Intelligence*. DOI: 10.1109/tpami.2020.3031625 61

Bak, Slawomir and Carr, Peter (2017). One-shot metric learning for person re-identification. In *Proc. of the IEEE Conference on Computer Vision and Pattern Recognition*, pages 2990–2999. DOI: 10.1109/cvpr.2017.171 6

Bąk, Sławomir, Corvee, Etienne, Bremond, Francois, and Thonnat, Monique (2012). Boosted human re-identification using Riemannian manifolds. *Image and Vision Computing*, 30(6-7):443–452. DOI: 10.1016/j.imavis.2011.08.008 3

Bazzani, Loris, Cristani, Marco, and Murino, Vittorio (2013a). Symmetry-driven accumulation of local features for human characterization and re-identification. *Computer Vision and Image Understanding*, 117(2):130–144. DOI: 10.1016/j.cviu.2012.10.008 3, 46, 47

Bazzani, Loris, Cristani, Marco, and Murino, Vittorio (2013b). Symmetry-driven accumulation of local features for human characterization and re-identification. *Computer Vision and Image Understanding*, 117(2):130–144. DOI: 10.1016/j.cviu.2012.10.008 15

Bendale, Abhijit and Boult, Terrance (2015). Towards open world recognition. In *CVPR*. DOI: 10.1109/cvpr.2015.7298799 7

Bengio, Yoshua, Léonard, Nicholas, and Courville, Aaron (2013). Estimating or propagating gradients through stochastic neurons for conditional computation. *ArXiv Preprint ArXiv:1308.3432*. 61

Biswas, Arijit and Parikh, Devi (2013). Simultaneous active learning of classifiers and attributes via relative feedback. In *IEEE Conference on Computer Vision and Pattern Recognition*. 6

Cancela, Brais, Hospedales, Timothy M., and Gong, Shaogang (2014). Open-world person re-identification by multi-label assignment inference. DOI: 10.5244/c.28.98 7

Cao, Min, Chen, Chen, Hu, Xiyuan, and Peng, Silong (2019). Towards fast and kernelized orthogonal discriminant analysis on person re-identification. *Pattern Recognition*, 94:218–229. DOI: 10.1016/j.patcog.2019.05.035 3

Chakraborty, Anirban, Das, Abir, and Roy-Chowdhury, Amit K. (2015). Network consistent data association. *IEEE Transactions on Pattern Analysis and Machine Intelligence*, 38(9):1859–1871. DOI: 10.1109/tpami.2015.2491922 4, 9, 32

Chakraborty, Anirban, Das, Abir, and Roy-Chowdhury, Amit K. (2016). Network consistent data association. *TPAMI*. DOI: 10.1109/tpami.2015.2491922 17

Chakraborty, Shayok, Balasubramanian, Vineeth N., and Panchanathan, Sethuraman (2011). Optimal batch selection for active learning in multi-label classification. In *ACM International Conference on Multimedia*, pages 1413–1416. DOI: 10.1145/2072298.2072028 6

Chen, Dapeng, Yuan, Zejian, Hua, Gang, Zheng, Nanning, and Wang, Jingdong (2015a). Similarity learning on an explicit polynomial Kernel feature map for person re-identification. In *International Conference on Computer Vision and Pattern Recognition*. DOI: 10.1109/cvpr.2015.7298764 4

Chen, Guangyi, Lin, Chunze, Ren, Liangliang, Lu, Jiwen, and Zhou, Jie (2019a). Self-critical attention learning for person re-identification. In *Proc. of the IEEE/CVF International Conference on Computer Vision*, pages 9637–9646. DOI: 10.1109/iccv.2019.00973 4

Chen, Guangyi, Lu, Jiwen, Yang, Ming, and Zhou, Jie (2019b). Spatial-temporal attention-aware learning for video-based person re-identification. *IEEE Transactions on Image Processing*, 28(9):4192–4205. DOI: 10.1109/tip.2019.2908062 25

Chen, Jiaxin, Zhang, Zhaoxiang, and Wang, Yunhong (2015b). Relevance Metric Learning for Person Re-Identification by Exploiting Listwise Similarities. *IEEE Transactions on Image Processing*, 7149(c):1–1. DOI: 10.1109/tip.2015.2466117 4

Chen, Mickaël and Denoyer, Ludovic (2017). Multi-view generative adversarial networks. In *Joint European Conference on Machine Learning and Knowledge Discovery in Databases*, pages 175–188, Springer. DOI: 10.1007/978-3-319-71246-8_11 58

Chen, Weihua, Chen, Xiaotang, Zhang, Jianguo, and Huang, Kaiqi (2017). Beyond triplet loss: A deep quadruplet network for person re-identification. In *Proc. of the IEEE Conference on Computer Vision and Pattern Recognition*, pages 403–412. DOI: 10.1109/cvpr.2017.145 4

Chen, Yanbei, Zhu, Xiatian, and Gong, Shaogang (2018). Deep association learning for unsupervised video person re-identification. In *Proc. of the British Machine Vision Conference (BMVC)*. 6, 30, 31, 38

Cheng, De, Gong, Yihong, Zhou, Sanping, Wang, Jinjun, and Zheng, Nanning (2016). Person re-identification by multi-channel parts-based CNN with improved triplet loss function. In *CVPR*. DOI: 10.1109/cvpr.2016.149 4

Cheng, Dong Seon, Cristani, Marco, Stoppa, Michele, Bazzani, Loris, and Murino, Vittorio (2011). Custom pictorial structures for re-identification. In *BMVC*. DOI: 10.5244/c.25.68 3, 5, 46, 47

Cheng, Yu, Wang, Duo, Zhou, Pan, and Zhang, Tao (2017). A survey of model compression and acceleration for deep neural networks. *ArXiv Preprint ArXiv:1710.09282*. 61

Choi, Yunjey, Choi, Minje, Kim, Munyoung, Ha, Jung-Woo, Kim, Sunghun, and Choo, Jaegul (2018). Stargan: Unified generative adversarial networks for multi-domain image-to-image translation. In *Proc. of the IEEE Conference on Computer Vision and Pattern Recognition*, pages 8789–8797. DOI: 10.1109/cvpr.2018.00916 5

Chu, Chun-Te and Hwang, Jenq-Neng (2014). Fully unsupervised learning of camera link models for tracking humans across nonoverlapping cameras. *IEEE Transactions on Circuits and Systems for Video Technology*, 24(6):979–994. DOI: 10.1109/tcsvt.2014.2302516 31

Cohen, Gilad, Sapiro, Guillermo, and Giryes, Raja (2020). Detecting adversarial samples using influence functions and nearest neighbors. In *Proc. of the IEEE/CVF Conference on Computer Vision and Pattern Recognition*, pages 14453–14462. DOI: 10.1109/cvpr42600.2020.01446 60

Das, Abir, Chakraborty, Anirban, and Roy-Chowdhury, Amit K. (2014). Consistent re-identification in a camera network. In *ECCV*. DOI: 10.1007/978-3-319-10605-2_22 4, 9, 17, 32, 36, 46, 53

Das, Abir, Panda, Rameswar, and Roy-Chowdhury, Amit (2015). Active image pair selection for continuous person re-identification. In *ICIP*. DOI: 10.1109/icip.2015.7351610 7, 59

Das, Abir, Panda, Rameswar, and Roy-Chowdhury, Amit K. (2017). Continuous adaptation of multi-camera person identification models through sparse non-redundant representative selection. *Computer Vision and Image Understanding*, 156:66–78. DOI: 10.1016/j.cviu.2016.10.012 7, 59

Daumé III, Hal (2009). Frustratingly easy domain adaptation. *ArXiv Preprint ArXiv:0907.1815.* 42

Ding, Chong, Bappy, Jawadul H., Farrell, Jay A., and Roy-Chowdhury, Amit K. (2016). Opportunistic image acquisition of individual and group activities in a distributed camera network. *IEEE Transactions on Circuits and Systems for Video Technology*, 27(3):664–672. DOI: 10.1109/tcsvt.2016.2593620 3

Ding, Chong, Song, Bi, Morye, Akshay, Farrell, Jay A., and Roy-Chowdhury, Amit K. (2012). Collaborative sensing in a distributed PTZ camera network. *IEEE Transactions on Image Processing*, 21(7):3282–3295. DOI: 10.1109/tip.2012.2188806 3

Du, Simon S, Koushik, Jayanth, Singh, Aarti, and Póczos, Barnabás (2017). Hypothesis transfer learning via transformation functions. In *Advances in Neural Information Processing Systems*, pages 574–584. 49, 53

Elhamifar, Ehsan, Sapiro, Guillermo, Yang, Allen, and Sasrty, Shankar S. (2013). A convex optimization framework for active learning. In *IEEE International Conference on Computer Vision*, pages 209–216. DOI: 10.1109/iccv.2013.33 6

Fan, Hehe, Zheng, Liang, Yan, Chenggang, and Yang, Yi (2018). Unsupervised person re-identification: Clustering and fine-tuning. *ACM Transactions on Multimedia Computing, Communications, and Applications*, 14(4):83:1–83:18. DOI: 10.1145/3243316 5

Fortmann, Thomas E., Bar-Shalom, Yaakov, and Scheffe, Molly (1980). Multi-target tracking using joint probabilistic data association. In *19th IEEE Conference on Decision and Control including the Symposium on Adaptive Processes*, pages 807–812. DOI: 10.1109/cdc.1980.271915 1

Fu, Yang, Wei, Yunchao, Wang, Guanshuo, Zhou, Yuqian, Shi, Honghui, and Huang, Thomas S. (2019). Self-similarity grouping: A simple unsupervised cross domain adaptation approach for person re-identification. In *Proc. of the IEEE International Conference on Computer Vision*, pages 6112–6121. DOI: 10.1109/iccv.2019.00621 31

García, Jorge, Martinel, Niki, Gardel, Alfredo, Bravo, Ignacio, Foresti, Gian Luca, and Micheloni, Christian (2016). Modeling feature distances by orientation driven classifiers for person re-identification. *Journal of Visual Communication and Image Representation*, 38:115–129. DOI: 10.1016/j.jvcir.2016.02.009 4

Geladi, Paul and Kowalski, Bruce R. (1986). Partial least-squares regression: A tutorial. *Analytica Chimica Acta*. DOI: 10.1016/0003-2670(86)80028-9 46

Gilbert, Andrew and Bowden, Richard (2006). Tracking objects across cameras by incrementally learning inter-camera colour calibration and patterns of activity. In *European Conference on Computer Vision*, pages 125–136, Springer. DOI: 10.1007/11744047_10 4

Gong, Boqing, Shi, Yuan, Sha, Fei, and Grauman, Kristen (2012). Geodesic flow kernel for unsupervised domain adaptation. In *CVPR*. DOI: 10.1109/cvpr.2012.6247911 44, 45, 47, 53

Gong, Shaogang, Cheng, Jian, Hou, Zengguang, et al. (2020). Faster person re-identification. In *European Conference on Computer Vision*, pages 275–292, Springer. DOI: 10.1007/978-3-030-58598-3_17 62

Gonzalez, Teofilo F. (2007). *Handbook of Approximation Algorithms and Metaheuristics*. CRC Press. DOI: 10.1201/9781420010749 21

Goodfellow, Ian J., Pouget-Abadie, Jean, Mirza, Mehdi, Xu, Bing, Warde-Farley, David, Ozair, Sherjil, Courville, Aaron, and Bengio, Yoshua (2014). Generative adversarial networks. *ArXiv Preprint ArXiv:1406.2661*. DOI: 10.1145/3422622 58

Gopalan, Raghuraman, Li, Ruonan, and Chellappa, Rama (2011). Domain adaptation for object recognition: An unsupervised approach. In *ICCV*. DOI: 10.1109/iccv.2011.6126344 42

Guo, Jianyuan, Yuan, Yuhui, Huang, Lang, Zhang, Chao, Yao, Jin-Ge, and Han, Kai (2019). Beyond human parts: Dual part-aligned representations for person re-identification. In *Proc. of the IEEE/CVF International Conference on Computer Vision*, pages 3642–3651. DOI: 10.1109/iccv.2019.00374 4

Guo, Yiluan and Cheung, Ngai-Man (2018). Efficient and deep person re-identification using multi-level similarity. In *Proc. of the IEEE Conference on Computer Vision and Pattern Recognition*, pages 2335–2344. DOI: 10.1109/cvpr.2018.00248 4

Hamid Rezatofighi, Seyed, Milan, Anton, Zhang, Zhen, Shi, Qinfeng, Dick, Anthony, and Reid, Ian (2016). Joint probabilistic matching using m-best solutions. In *Proc. of the IEEE Conference on Computer Vision and Pattern Recognition*, pages 136–145. DOI: 10.1109/cvpr.2016.22 6

Hasan, Mahmudul, Paul, Sujoy, Mourikis, Anastasios I., and Roy-Chowdhury, Amit K. (2018). Context-aware query selection for active learning in event recognition. *IEEE Transactions on Pattern Analysis and Machine Intelligence*, 42(3):554–567. DOI: 10.1109/tpami.2018.2878696 6

He, Lingxiao, Liang, Jian, Li, Haiqing, and Sun, Zhenan (2018). Deep spatial feature reconstruction for partial person re-identification: Alignment-free approach. In *Proc. of the IEEE Conference on Computer Vision and Pattern Recognition*, pages 7073–7082. DOI: 10.1109/cvpr.2018.00739 7

Hirzer, Martin, Roth, Peter M., Martin, K., and Bischof, Horst (2012). Relaxed pairwise learned metric for person re-identification. In *European Conference Computer Vision*, volume 7577 of *Lecture Notes in Computer Science*, pages 780–793. DOI: 10.1007/978-3-642-33783-3_56 1, 3

Hussain, Tanveer, Muhammad, Khan, Ding, Weiping, Lloret, Jaime, Baik, Sung Wook, and de Albuquerque, Victor Hugo C. (2021). A comprehensive survey of multi-view video summarization. *Pattern Recognition*, 109:107567. DOI: 10.1016/j.patcog.2020.107567 3

Hussain, Tanveer, Muhammad, Khan, Ullah, Amin, Cao, Zehong, Baik, Sung Wook, and de Albuquerque, Victor Hugo C. (2019). Cloud-assisted multiview video summarization using CNN and bidirectional LSTM. *IEEE Transactions on Industrial Informatics*, 16(1):77–86. DOI: 10.1109/tii.2019.2929228 3

Huynh, Su V. (2021). A strong baseline for vehicle re-identification. In *Proc. of the IEEE/CVF Conference on Computer Vision and Pattern Recognition*, pages 4147–4154. 1

Javed, Omar, Shafique, Khurram, Rasheed, Zeeshan, and Shah, Mubarak (2008a). Modeling inter-camera space-time and appearance relationships for tracking across non-overlapping views. *Computer Vision and Image Understanding*, 109(2):146–162. DOI: 10.1016/j.cviu.2007.01.003 4

Javed, Omar, Shafique, Khurram, Rasheed, Zeeshan, and Shah, Mubarak (2008b). Modeling inter-camera space-time and appearance relationships for tracking across non-overlapping views. *Computer Vision and Image Understanding*, 109(2):146–162. DOI: 10.1016/j.cviu.2007.01.003 14

Jie, Luo, Tommasi, Tatiana, and Caputo, Barbara (2011). Multiclass transfer learning from unconstrained priors. In *ICCV*. DOI: 10.1109/iccv.2011.6126454 42

Joshi, Ajay J., Porikli, Fatih, and Papanikolopoulos, Nikolaos P. (2012). Scalable active learning for multiclass image classification. *IEEE Transactions on Pattern Analysis and Machine Intelligence*, 34(11):2259–2273. DOI: 10.1109/tpami.2012.21 6

Kamal, Ahmed T., Bappy, Jawadul H., Farrell, Jay A., and Roy-Chowdhury, Amit K. (2015). Distributed multi-target tracking and data association in vision networks. *IEEE Transactions on Pattern Analysis and Machine Intelligence*, 38(7):1397–1410. DOI: 10.1109/tpami.2015.2484339 3

Kamal, Ahmed T., Farrell, Jay A., and Roy-Chowdhury, Amit K. (2013). Information consensus for distributed multi-target tracking. In *Proc. of the IEEE Conference on Computer Vision and Pattern Recognition*, pages 2403–2410. DOI: 10.1109/cvpr.2013.311 3

Kamal, A. T., Ding, C., Morye, A. A., Farrell, J. A., and Roy-Chowdhury, Amit K. (2014). An overview of distributed tracking and control in camera networks. *Wide Area Surveillance*, pages 207–234. DOI: 10.1007/8612_2012_10 3

Karanam, Srikrishna, Li, Yang, and Radke, Richard J. (2015). Person re-identification with discriminatively trained viewpoint invariant dictionaries. In *ICCV*. DOI: 10.1109/iccv.2015.513 3, 46

Khan, Furqan M. and Bremond, Francois (2016). Unsupervised data association for metric learning in the context of multi-shot person re-identification. In *Proc. of IEEE International Conference on Advanced Video and Signal Based Surveillance*, pages 256–262. DOI: 10.1109/avss.2016.7738058 38

Kodirov, Elyor, Xiang, Tao, Fu, Zhenyong, and Gong, Shaogang (2016). Person re-identification by unsupervised\ell _1 graph learning. In *ECCV*. DOI: 10.1007/978-3-319-46448-0_11 5, 37, 38, 46

Koestinger, Martin, Hirzer, Martin, Wohlhart, Paul, Roth, Peter M., and Bischof, Horst (2012). Large scale metric learning from equivalence constraints. In *CVPR*, pages 2288–2295, IEEE. DOI: 10.1109/cvpr.2012.6247939 3

Kolesnikov, Alexander, Zhai, Xiaohua, and Beyer, Lucas (2019). Revisiting self-supervised visual representation learning. *ArXiv Preprint ArXiv:1901.09005*. DOI: 10.1109/cvpr.2019.00202 26

Kostinger, M., Hirzer, Martin, Wohlhart, Paul, Roth, Peter M., and Bischof, Horst (2012). Large scale metric learning from equivalence constraints. In *International Conference on Computer Vision and Pattern Recognition*, pages 2288–2295. DOI: 10.1109/cvpr.2012.6247939 4

Köstinger, Martin, Hirzer, Martin, Wohlhart, Paul, Roth, Peter M., and Bischof, Horst (2012). Large scale metric learning from equivalence constraints. In *CVPR*. DOI: 10.1109/cvpr.2012.6247939 22, 43, 44, 46

Kou, Gang, Ergu, Daji, and Shang, Jennifer (2014). Enhancing data consistency in decision matrix: Adapting Hadamard model to mitigate judgment contradiction. *European Journal of Operational Research*. DOI: 10.1016/j.ejor.2013.11.035 45

Kuhn, Harold W. (1955). The Hungarian method for the assignment problem. *Naval Research Logistics Quarterly*, 2(1–2):83–97. DOI: 10.1002/nav.3800020109 35

Kulis, Brian, Saenko, Kate, and Darrell, Trevor (2011). What you saw is not what you get: Domain adaptation using asymmetric kernel transforms. In *CVPR*. DOI: 10.1109/cvpr.2011.5995702 42

Kurakin, Alexey, Goodfellow, Ian, and Bengio, Samy (2016). Adversarial machine learning at scale. *ArXiv Preprint ArXiv:1611.01236*. 60

Kuzborskij, Ilja and Orabona, Francesco (2013). Stability and hypothesis transfer learning. In *ICML*, pages 942–950. 51, 53

Kviatkovsky, Igor, Adam, Amit, and Rivlin, Ehud (2012). Color invariants for person re-identification. *IEEE Transactions on Pattern Analysis and Machine Intelligence*, 35(7):1622–1634. DOI: 10.1109/tpami.2012.246 3

Layne, Ryan, Hospedales, Timothy M., and Gong, Shaogang (2014). Investigating open-world person re-identification using a drone. In *European Conference on Computer Vision*, pages 225–240, Springer. DOI: 10.1007/978-3-319-16199-0_16 7

Leng, Qingming, Ye, Mang, and Tian, Qi (2019). A survey of open-world person re-identification. *IEEE Transactions on Circuits and Systems for Video Technology*, 30(4):1092–1108. DOI: 10.1109/tcsvt.2019.2898940 7

Li, Diangang, Gong, Yihong, Cheng, De, Shi, Weiwei, Tao, Xiaoyu, and Chang, Xinyuan (2019a). Consistency-preserving deep hashing for fast person re-identification. *Pattern Recognition*, 94:207–217. DOI: 10.1016/j.patcog.2019.05.036 3

Li, Minxian, Zhu, Xiatian, and Gong, Shaogang (2018a). Unsupervised person re-identification by deep learning tracklet association. In *Proc. of the European Conference on Computer Vision*, pages 737–753. DOI: 10.1007/978-3-030-01225-0_45 5, 38

Li, Minxian, Zhu, Xiatian, and Gong, Shaogang (2019b). Unsupervised tracklet person re-identification. *IEEE Transactions on Pattern Analysis and Machine Intelligence.* DOI: 10.1109/tpami.2019.2903058 5, 30, 31, 38

Li, Peike, Panb, Pingbo, Liuc, Ping, Xu, Mingliang, and Yang, Yi (2020a). Hierarchical temporal modeling with mutual distance matching for video based person re-identification. *IEEE Transactions on Circuits and Systems for Video Technology.* DOI: 10.1109/tcsvt.2020.2988034 25

Li, Shasha, Zhu, Shitong, Paul, Sudipta, Roy-Chowdhury, Amit, Song, Chengyu, Krishnamurthy, Srikanth, Swami, Ananthram, and Chan, Kevin S. (2020b). Connecting the dots: Detecting adversarial perturbations using context inconsistency. In *European Conference on Computer Vision*, pages 396–413, Springer. DOI: 10.1007/978-3-030-58592-1_24 60

Li, Wei, Zhao, Rui, Xiao, Tong, and Wang, Xiaogang (2014). DeepReID: Deep filter pairing neural network for person re-identification. In *CVPR*. DOI: 10.1109/cvpr.2014.27 4

Li, Wei, Zhu, Xiatian, and Gong, Shaogang (2018b). Harmonious attention network for person re-identification. In *Proc. of the IEEE Conference on Computer Vision and Pattern Recognition*, pages 2285–2294. DOI: 10.1109/cvpr.2018.00243 4

Li, Xiang, Wu, Ancong, and Zheng, Wei-Shi (2018c). Adversarial open-world person re-identification. In *Proc. of the European Conference on Computer Vision (ECCV)*, pages 280–296. DOI: 10.1007/978-3-030-01216-8_18 7

Li, Zhen, Chang, Shiyu, Liang, Feng, Huang, Thomas S., Cao, Liangliang, and Smith, John R. (2013). Learning locally-adaptive decision functions for person verification. In *International Conference on Computer Vision and Pattern Recognition*, pages 3610–3617, IEEE. DOI: 10.1109/cvpr.2013.463 4

Liao, Shengcai, Hu, Yang, Zhu, Xiangyu, and Li, Stan Z. (2015a). Person re-identification by local maximal occurrence representation and metric learning. In *CVPR*. DOI: 10.1109/cvpr.2015.7298832 2, 4

Liao, Shengcai, Hu, Yang, Zhu, Xiangyu, and Li, Stan Z. (2015b). Person re-identification by local maximal occurrence representation and metric learning. In *CVPR*. DOI: 10.1109/cvpr.2015.7298832 3, 37

Liao, Shengcai, Hu, Yang, Zhu, Xiangyu, and Li, Stan Z. (2015c). Person re-identification by local maximal occurrence representation and metric learning. In *International Conference on Computer Vision and Pattern Recognition*. DOI: 10.1109/cvpr.2015.7298832 4

Liao, Shengcai and Li, Stan Z. (2015a). Efficient PSD constrained asymmetric metric learning for person re-identification. In *International Conference on Computer Vision*, pages 3685–3693. DOI: 10.1109/iccv.2015.420 1, 4

Liao, Shengcai and Li, Stan Z. (2015b). Efficient PSD constrained asymmetric metric learning for person re-identification. In *ICCV*. DOI: 10.1109/iccv.2015.420 3, 37

Lin, Ji, Ren, Liangliang, Lu, Jiwen, Feng, Jianjiang, and Zhou, Jie (2017). Consistent-aware deep learning for person re-identification in a camera network. In *Proc. of the IEEE Conference on Computer Vision and Pattern Recognition*, pages 5771–5780. DOI: 10.1109/cvpr.2017.362 5

Lin, Yutian, Dong, Xuanyi, Zheng, Liang, Yan, Yan, and Yang, Yi (2019a). A bottom-up clustering approach to unsupervised person re-identification. In *AAAI*, 33:8738–8745. DOI: 10.1609/aaai.v33i01.33018738 5, 6, 30, 31, 37, 38

Lin, Yutian, Xie, Lingxi, Wu, Yu, Yan, Chenggang, and Tian, Qi (2020). Unsupervised person re-identification via softened similarity learning. In *Proc. of the IEEE/CVF Conference on Computer Vision and Pattern Recognition*, pages 3390–3399. DOI: 10.1109/cvpr42600.2020.00345 31, 38, 39

Lin, Yutian, Zheng, Liang, Zheng, Zhedong, Wu, Yu, Hu, Zhilan, Yan, Chenggang, and Yang, Yi (2019b). Improving person re-identification by attribute and identity learning. *Pattern Recognition*, 95:151–161. DOI: 10.1016/j.patcog.2019.06.006 4

Lisanti, Giuseppe, Masi, Iacopo, Bagdanov, Andrew D., and Del Bimbo, Alberto (2015). Person re-identification by iterative re-weighted sparse ranking. *TPAMI*. DOI: 10.1109/tpami.2014.2369055 22, 46, 53

Liu, Chunxiao, Gong, Shaogang, and Loy, Chen Change (2014a). On-the-fly feature importance mining for person re-identification. *Pattern Recognition*. DOI: 10.1016/j.patcog.2013.11.001 5

Liu, Chunxiao, Gong, Shaogang, Loy, Chen Change, and Lin, Xinggang (2012). Person re-identification: What features are important? In *European Conference on Computer Vision*, pages 391–401, Springer. DOI: 10.1007/978-3-642-33863-2_39 3

Liu, Chunxiao, Loy, Chen Change, Gong, Shaogang, and Wang, Guijin (2013). Pop: Person re-identification post-rank optimisation. In *Proc. of the IEEE International Conference on Computer Vision*, pages 441–448. DOI: 10.1109/iccv.2013.62 7

Liu, Xiao, Song, Mingli, Tao, Dacheng, Zhou, Xingchen, Chen, Chun, and Bu, Jiajun (2014b). Semi-supervised coupled dictionary learning for person re-identification. In *CVPR*. DOI: 10.1109/cvpr.2014.454 6

Liu, Xinchen, Liu, Wu, Ma, Huadong, and Fu, Huiyuan (2016a). Large-scale vehicle re-identification in urban surveillance videos. In *2016 IEEE International Conference on Multimedia and Expo (ICME)*, pages 1–6. DOI: 10.1109/icme.2016.7553002 1

Liu, Xinchen, Liu, Wu, Mei, Tao, and Ma, Huadong (2016b). A deep learning-based approach to progressive vehicle re-identification for urban surveillance. In *European Conference on Computer Vision*, pages 869–884, Springer. DOI: 10.1007/978-3-319-46475-6_53 1

Liu, Zimo, Wang, Dong, and Lu, Huchuan (2017). Stepwise metric promotion for unsupervised video person re-identification. In *Proc. of the IEEE International Conference on Computer Vision*, pages 2429–2438. DOI: 10.1109/iccv.2017.266 5, 6, 30, 31, 38

Liu, Zimo, Wang, Jingya, Gong, Shaogang, Lu, Huchuan, and Tao, Dacheng (2019). Deep reinforcement active learning for human-in-the-loop person re-identification. In *Proc. of the IEEE/CVF International Conference on Computer Vision*, pages 6122–6131. DOI: 10.1109/iccv.2019.00622 7

Luo, Hao, Jiang, Wei, Zhang, Xuan, Fan, Xing, Qian, Jingjing, and Zhang, Chi (2019). AlignedReID++: Dynamically matching local information for person re-identification. *Pattern Recognition*, 94:53–61. DOI: 10.1016/j.patcog.2019.05.028 4

Ma, Bingpeng, Su, Yu, and Jurie, Frédéric (2012). Bicov: A novel image representation for person re-identification and face verification. In *British Machine Vision Conference*, page 11–pages. DOI: 10.5244/c.26.57 3

Ma, Zhigang, Yang, Yi, Nie, Feiping, Sebe, Nicu, Yan, Shuicheng, and Hauptmann, Alexander G. (2014). Harnessing lab knowledge for real-world action recognition. *IJCV*. DOI: 10.1007/s11263-014-0717-5 42

Marchand, Hugues, Martin, Alexander, Weismantel, Robert, and Wolsey, Laurence (2002). Cutting planes in integer and mixed integer programming. *Discrete Applied Mathematics*. DOI: 10.1016/s0166-218x(01)00348-1 17, 21

Martinel, Niki, Das, Abir, Micheloni, Christian, and Roy-Chowdhury, Amit K. (2015). Re-identification in the function space of feature warps. *TPAMI*. DOI: 10.1109/tpami.2014.2377748 3

Martinel, Niki, Das, Abir, Micheloni, Christian, and Roy-Chowdhury, Amit K. (2016). Temporal model adaptation for person re-identification. In *ECCV*. DOI: 10.1007/978-3-319-46493-0_52 7, 46, 59

Martinel, Niki and Micheloni, Christian (2012a). Re-identify people in wide area camera network. In *IEEE Computer Society Conference on Computer Vision and Pattern Recognition Workshops*, pages 31–36. DOI: 10.1109/cvprw.2012.6239203 3

Martinel, Niki and Micheloni, Christian (2012b). Re-identify people in wide area camera network. In *Computer Vision and Pattern Recognition Workshops*, pages 31–36, Providence, RI. DOI: 10.1109/cvprw.2012.6239203 14, 15

Martinel, Niki and Micheloni, Christian (2015). Classification of local Eigen-dissimilarities for person re-identification. *IEEE Signal Processing Letters*, 22(4):455–459. DOI: 10.1109/lsp.2014.2362573 4

Meng, Jingke, Wu, Ancong, and Zheng, Wei-Shi (2019a). Deep asymmetric video-based person re-identification. *Pattern Recognition*, 93:430–441. DOI: 10.1016/j.patcog.2019.04.008 4

Meng, Jingke, Wu, Sheng, and Zheng, Wei-Shi (2019b). Weakly supervised person re-identification. In *Proc. of the IEEE/CVF Conference on Computer Vision and Pattern Recognition*, pages 760–769. DOI: 10.1109/cvpr.2019.00085 6

Meng, Yue, Lin, Chung-Ching, Panda, Rameswar, Sattigeri, Prasanna, Karlinsky, Leonid, Oliva, Aude, Saenko, Kate, and Feris, Rogerio (2020). Ar-Net: Adaptive frame resolution for efficient action recognition. In *European Conference on Computer Vision*, pages 86–104, Springer. DOI: 10.1007/978-3-030-58571-6_6 61

Michael, R. Garey and David, S. Johnson (1979). *Computers and Intractability: A Guide to the Theory of NP-Completeness*. WH Free. Co., San Francisco, CO. 21

Misra, Ishan, Zitnick, C. Lawrence, and Hebert, Martial (2016). Shuffle and learn: Unsupervised learning using temporal order verification. In *European Conference on Computer Vision*, pages 527–544, Springer. DOI: 10.1007/978-3-319-46448-0_32 26

Mitchell, John E. (2002). Branch-and-cut algorithms for combinatorial optimization problems. *Handbook of Applied Optimization*. 17, 21

Mithun, Niluthpol Chowdhury, Panda, Rameswar, and Roy-Chowdhury, Amit K. (2016). Generating diverse image datasets with limited labeling. In *Proc. of the 24th ACM International Conference on Multimedia*, pages 566–570. DOI: 10.1145/2964284.2967285 6

Mitzenmacher, Michael and Upfal, Eli (2017). *Probability and Computing: Randomization and Probabilistic Techniques in Algorithms and Data Analysis*. Cambridge University Press. 21

Mobahi, Hossein, Collobert, Ronan, and Weston, Jason (2009). Deep learning from temporal coherence in video. In *Proc. of the 26th Annual International Conference on Machine Learning*, pages 737–744, ACM. DOI: 10.1145/1553374.1553469 26

Paisitkriangkrai, Sakrapee, Shen, Chunhua, and Hengel, Anton Van Den (2015a). Learning to rank in person re-identification with metric ensembles. In *International Conference on Computer Vision and Pattern Recognition*. DOI: 10.1109/cvpr.2015.7298794 2, 4

Paisitkriangkrai, Sakrapee, Shen, Chunhua, and Van Den Hengel, Anton (2015b). Learning to rank in person re-identification with metric ensembles. In *CVPR*. DOI: 10.1109/cvpr.2015.7298794 46

Panda, Rameswar, Bhuiyan, Amran, Murino, Vittorio, and Roy-Chowdhury, Amit K. (2017a). Unsupervised adaptive re-identification in open world dynamic camera networks. In *CVPR*. DOI: 10.1109/cvpr.2017.151 7, 41, 43, 53

Panda, Rameswar, Bhuiyan, Amran, Murino, Vittorio, and Roy-Chowdhury, Amit K. (2019). Adaptation of person re-identification models for on-boarding new camera (s). *Pattern Recognition*, 96:106991. DOI: 10.1016/j.patcog.2019.106991 7, 41, 53

Panda, Rameswar, Dasy, Abir, and Roy-Chowdhury, Amit K. (2016). Video summarization in a multi-view camera network. In *23rd International Conference on Pattern Recognition (ICPR)*, pages 2971–2976, IEEE. DOI: 10.1109/icpr.2016.7900089 3

Panda, Rameswar, Mithun, Niluthpol Chowdhury, and Roy-Chowdhury, Amit K. (2017b). Diversity-aware multi-video summarization. *IEEE Transactions on Image Processing*, 26(10):4712–4724. DOI: 10.1109/tip.2017.2708902 3

Panda, Rameswar and Roy-Chowdhury, Amit K. (2017). Multi-view surveillance video summarization via joint embedding and sparse optimization. *IEEE Transactions on Multimedia*, 19(9):2010–2021. DOI: 10.1109/tmm.2017.2708981 3

Paul, Sujoy, Bappy, Jawadul H., and Roy-Chowdhury, Amit K. (2017). Non-uniform subset selection for active learning in structured data. In *Proc. of the IEEE Conference on Computer Vision and Pattern Recognition*, pages 6846–6855. DOI: 10.1109/cvpr.2017.95 6

Paul, Sujoy, Roy, Sourya, and Roy-Chowdhury, Amit K. (2018). Incorporating scalability in unsupervised spatio-temporal feature learning. In *IEEE International Conference on Acoustics, Speech and Signal Processing (ICASSP)*, pages 1503–1507. DOI: 10.1109/icassp.2018.8461758 26

Pedagadi, Sateesh, Orwell, James, and Velastin, Sergio (2013). Local fisher discriminant analysis for pedestrian re-identification. In *International Conference on Computer Vision and Pattern Recognition*, pages 3318–3325. DOI: 10.1109/cvpr.2013.426 4

Phillips, Jeff M. and Venkatasubramanian, Suresh (2011). A gentle introduction to the kernel distance. *ArXiv Preprint ArXiv:1103.1625*. 45, 46

Qian, Xuelin, Fu, Yanwei, Jiang, Yu-Gang, Xiang, Tao, and Xue, Xiangyang (2017). Multi-scale deep learning architectures for person re-identification. In *Proc. of the IEEE International Conference on Computer Vision*, pages 5399–5408. DOI: 10.1109/iccv.2017.577 4

Quan, Ruijie, Dong, Xuanyi, Wu, Yu, Zhu, Linchao, and Yang, Yi (2019). Auto-ReID: Searching for a part-aware convnet for person re-identification. In *Proc. of the IEEE/CVF International Conference on Computer Vision*, pages 3750–3759. DOI: 10.1109/iccv.2019.00385 61, 62

Rao, Yongming, Lu, Jiwen, and Zhou, Jie (2019). Learning discriminative aggregation network for video-based face recognition and person re-identification. *International Journal of Computer Vision*, 127(6–7):701–718. DOI: 10.1007/s11263-018-1135-x 25

Raychaudhuri, Dripta S. and Roy-Chowdhury, Amit K. (2020). Exploiting temporal coherence for self-supervised one-shot video re-identification. In *Computer Vision—ECCV: 16th European Conference, Proceedings*, Glasgow, UK, August 23–28. DOI: 10.1007/978-3-030-58583-9_16 6, 25, 38

Riachy, Chirine, Khelifi, Fouad, and Bouridane, Ahmed (2019). Video-based person re-identification using unsupervised tracklet matching. *IEEE Access*, 7:20596–20606. DOI: 10.1109/access.2019.2896779 38

Ristani, Ergys, Solera, Francesco, Zou, Roger, Cucchiara, Rita, and Tomasi, Carlo (2016). Performance measures and a data set for multi-target, multi-camera tracking. In *European Conference on Computer Vision*, pages 17–35, Springer. DOI: 10.1007/978-3-319-48881-3_2 3

Ristani, Ergys and Tomasi, Carlo (2018). Features for multi-target multi-camera tracking and re-identification. In *Proc. of the IEEE Conference on Computer Vision and Pattern Recognition*, pages 6036–6046. DOI: 10.1109/cvpr.2018.00632 3

Roth, D. (2017). Incidental supervision: Moving beyond supervised learning. In *AAAI*. 2

Roy, Sourya, Paul, Sujoy, Young, Neal E., and Roy-Chowdhury, Amit K. (2018). Exploiting transitivity for learning person re-identification models on a budget. In *Proc. of the IEEE Conference on Computer Vision and Pattern Recognition*, pages 7064–7072. DOI: 10.1109/cvpr.2018.00738 7, 9, 17, 23

Roy-Chowdhury, Amit K. and Song, Bi (2012). Camera networks: The acquisition and analysis of videos over wide areas. *Synthesis Lectures on Computer Vision*, 3(1):1–133. DOI: 10.2200/s00400ed1v01y201201cov004 3

Saenko, Kate, Kulis, Brian, Fritz, Mario, and Darrell, Trevor (2010). Adapting visual category models to new domains. In *ECCV*. DOI: 10.1007/978-3-642-15561-1_16 42, 43

Sarfraz, Saquib, Sharma, Vivek, and Stiefelhagen, Rainer (2019). Efficient parameter-free clustering using first neighbor relations. In *Proc. of the IEEE Conference on Computer Vision and Pattern Recognition*, pages 8934–8943. DOI: 10.1109/cvpr.2019.00914 32

Schrijver, Alexander (1998). *Theory of Linear and Integer Programming*. John Wiley & Sons. 11

Schwartz, William Robson, Kembhavi, Aniruddha, Harwood, David, and Davis, Larry S. (2009). Human detection using partial least squares analysis. In *ICCV*. DOI: 10.1109/iccv.2009.5459205 46

Settles, Burr (2012). Active learning. *Synthesis Lectures on Artificial Intelligence and Machine Learning*, 6(1):1–114. DOI: 10.2200/s00429ed1v01y201207aim018 6

Song, Bi, Ding, Chong, Kamal, Ahmed T., Farrell, Jay A., and Roy-Chowdhury, Amit K. (2011). Distributed camera networks. *IEEE Signal Processing Magazine*, 28(3):20–31. DOI: 10.1109/msp.2011.940441 3

Song, Bi, Kamal, Ahmed T., Soto, Cristian, Ding, Chong, Farrell, Jay A., and Roy-Chowdhury, Amit K. (2010). Tracking and activity recognition through consensus in distributed camera networks. *IEEE Transactions on Image Processing*, 19(10):2564–2579. DOI: 10.1109/tip.2010.2052823 3

Song, Jifei, Yang, Yongxin, Song, Yi-Zhe, Xiang, Tao, and Hospedales, Timothy M. (2019). Generalizable person re-identification by domain-invariant mapping network. In *Proc. of the IEEE/CVF Conference on Computer Vision and Pattern Recognition*, pages 719–728. DOI: 10.1109/cvpr.2019.00081 58

Tan, Mingxing and Le, Quoc (2019). EfficientNet: Rethinking model scaling for convolutional neural networks. In *International Conference on Machine Learning*, pages 6105–6114, PMLR. 61

Tao, Dapeng, Jin, Lianwen, Wang, Yongfei, and Li, Xuelong (2014). Person re-identification by minimum classification error-based KISS metric learning. *IEEE Transactions on Cybernetics*, pages 1–11. 4

Tao, Dapeng, Jin, Lianwen, Wang, Yongfei, Yuan, Yuan, and Li, Xuelong (2013). Person re-identification by regularized smoothing KISS metric learning. *IEEE Transactions on Circuits and Systems for Video Technology*, 23(10):1675–1685. DOI: 10.1109/tcsvt.2013.2255413 4

Tramèr, Florian, Kurakin, Alexey, Papernot, Nicolas, Goodfellow, Ian, Boneh, Dan, and McDaniel, Patrick (2017). Ensemble adversarial training: Attacks and defenses. *ArXiv Preprint ArXiv:1705.07204*. 60

Van Engelen, Jesper E. and Hoos, Holger H. (2020). A survey on semi-supervised learning. *Machine Learning*, 109(2):373–440. DOI: 10.1007/s10994-019-05855-6 2

Wang, Hanxiao, Gong, Shaogang, and Xiang, Tao (2016a). Highly efficient regression for scalable person re-identification. *ArXiv Preprint ArXiv:1612.01341*. DOI: 10.5244/c.30.134 7

Wang, Hanxiao, Gong, Shaogang, Zhu, Xiatian, and Xiang, Tao (2016b). Human-in-the-loop person re-identification. In *ECCV*. DOI: 10.1007/978-3-319-46493-0_25 7, 59

Wang, Xueping, Li, Shasha, Liu, Min, Wang, Yaonan, and Roy-Chowdhury, Amit K. (2021a). Spatio-temporal representation factorization for video-based person re-identification. In *Proc. of the IEEE International Conference on Computer Vision*. 61

Wang, Xueping, Liu, Min, Raychaudhuri, Dripta S., Paul, Sujoy, Wang, Yaonan, and Roy-Chowdhury, Amit K. (2021b). Learning person re-identification models from videos with weak supervision. *IEEE Transactions on Image Processing*, 30:3017–3028. DOI: 10.1109/tip.2021.3056223 6, 25

Wang, Xueping, Panda, Rameswar, Liu, Min, Wang, Yaonan, and Roy-Chowdhury, Amit K. (2020a). Exploiting global camera network constraints for unsupervised video person re-identification. *IEEE Transactions on Circuits and Systems for Video Technology*. DOI: 10.1109/tcsvt.2020.3043444 5

Wang, Xueping, Paul, Sujoy, Raychaudhuri, Dripta S., Liu, Min, Wang, Yaonan, Roy-Chowdhury, Amit K., et al. (2020b). Learning person re-identification models from videos with weak supervision. *ArXiv Preprint ArXiv:2007.10631*. DOI: 10.1109/tip.2021.3056223 25

Wang, Yan, Wang, Lequn, You, Yurong, Zou, Xu, Chen, Vincent, Li, Serena, Huang, Gao, Hariharan, Bharath, and Weinberger, Kilian Q. (2018). Resource aware person re-identification across multiple resolutions. In *Proc. of the IEEE Conference on Computer Vision and Pattern Recognition*, pages 8042–8051. DOI: 10.1109/cvpr.2018.00839 61

Wang, Zheng, Hu, Ruimin, Liang, Chao, Leng, Qingming, and Sun, Kaimin (2014). Region-based interactive ranking optimization for person re-identification. In *Pacific Rim Conference on Multimedia*, pages 1–10, Springer. DOI: 10.1007/978-3-319-13168-9_1 7

Wang, Zhibo, Zheng, Siyan, Song, Mengkai, Wang, Qian, Rahimpour, Alireza, and Qi, Hairong (2019). Advpattern: Physical-world attacks on deep person re-identification via adversarially transformable patterns. In *Proc. of the IEEE/CVF International Conference on Computer Vision*, pages 8341–8350. DOI: 10.1109/iccv.2019.00843 61

Weinberger, Kilian Q. and Saul, Lawrence K. (2009). Distance metric learning for large margin nearest neighbor classification. *JMLR*. 4

Wold, Svante, Esbensen, Kim, and Geladi, Paul (1987). Principal component analysis. *Chemometrics and Intelligent Laboratory Systems*, 2(1–3):37–52. DOI: 10.1016/0169-7439(87)80084-9 37

Wu, Guile, Zhu, Xiatian, and Gong, Shaogang (2020). Tracklet self-supervised learning for unsupervised person re-identification. In *Proc. of AAAI Conference on Artificial Intelligence*, pages 12362–12369. DOI: 10.1609/aaai.v34i07.6921 25, 38

Wu, Jinlin, Yang, Yang, Liu, Hao, Liao, Shengcai, Lei, Zhen, and Li, Stan Z. (2019a). Unsupervised graph association for person re-identification. In *Proc. of the IEEE International Conference on Computer Vision*, pages 8321–8330. DOI: 10.1109/iccv.2019.00841 5, 38

Wu, Yu, Lin, Yutian, Dong, Xuanyi, Yan, Yan, Bian, Wei, and Yang, Yi (2019b). Progressive learning for person re-identification with one example. *IEEE Transactions on Image Processing*, 28(6):2872–2881. DOI: 10.1109/tip.2019.2891895 6, 26, 30, 31, 38

Wu, Yu, Lin, Yutian, Dong, Xuanyi, Yan, Yan, Ouyang, Wanli, and Yang, Yi (2018a). Exploit the unknown gradually: One-shot video-based person re-identification by stepwise learning. In *The IEEE Conference on Computer Vision and Pattern Recognition (CVPR)*. DOI: 10.1109/cvpr.2018.00543 6, 26, 30, 31

Wu, Yu, Lin, Yutian, Dong, Xuanyi, Yan, Yan, Ouyang, Wanli, and Yang, Yi (2018b). Exploit the unknown gradually: One-shot video-based person re-identification by stepwise learning. In *CVPR*, pages 5177–5186. DOI: 10.1109/cvpr.2018.00543 38

Wu, Ziyan, Li, Y, and Radke, Richard J. (2016). Viewpoint invariant human re-identification in camera networks using pose priors and subject-discriminative features. *TPAMI*. DOI: 10.1109/tpami.2014.2360373 3

Xiao, Tong, Li, Hongsheng, Ouyang, Wanli, and Wang, Xiaogang (2016). Learning deep feature representations with domain guided dropout for person re-identification. *ArXiv Preprint ArXiv:1604.07528*. DOI: 10.1109/cvpr.2016.140 4

Xiao, Tong, Li, Shuang, Wang, Bochao, Lin, Liang, and Wang, Xiaogang (2017). Joint detection and identification feature learning for person search. In *Proc. of the IEEE Conference on Computer Vision and Pattern Recognition*, pages 3415–3424. DOI: 10.1109/cvpr.2017.360 5, 38

Xie, Qizhe, Luong, Minh-Thang, Hovy, Eduard, and Le, Quoc V. (2020). Self-training with noisy student improves imagenet classification. In *Proc. of the IEEE/CVF Conference on Computer Vision and Pattern Recognition*, pages 10687–10698. DOI: 10.1109/cvpr42600.2020.01070 2

Xing, Eric P., Ng, Andrew Y., Jordan, Michael I., and Russell, Stuart (2002). Distance metric learning, with application to clustering with side-information. *Advances in Neural Information Processing Systems*, 15:505–512. 1, 3

Xiong, Fei, Gou, Mengran, Camps, Octavia, and Sznaier, Mario (2014).   Person re-identification using kernel-based metric learning methods. In *ECCV*. DOI: 10.1007/978-3-319-10584-0_1 2, 4

Yalniz, I. Zeki, Jégou, Hervé, Chen, Kan, Paluri, Manohar, and Mahajan, Dhruv (2019).   Billion-scale semi-supervised learning for image classification. *ArXiv Preprint ArXiv:1905.00546.* 2

Yang, Fan, Yan, Ke, Lu, Shijian, Jia, Huizhu, Xie, Xiaodong, and Gao, Wen (2019). Attention driven person re-identification.   *Pattern Recognition*, 86:143–155. DOI: 10.1016/j.patcog.2018.08.015 4

Yang, Yi, Ma, Zhigang, Xu, Zhongwen, Yan, Shuicheng, and Hauptmann, Alexander G. (2013). How related exemplars help complex event detection in web videos? In *ICCV*. DOI: 10.1109/iccv.2013.456 42

Ye, M., Li, J., Ma, A. J., Zheng, L., and Yuen, P. C. (2019). Dynamic graph co-matching for unsupervised video-based person re-identification. *IEEE Transactions on Image Processing*, 28(6):2976–2990. DOI: 10.1109/tip.2019.2893066 5, 38

Ye, Mang, Lan, Xiangyuan, Leng, Qingming, and Shen, Jianbing (2020a). Cross-modality person re-identification via modality-aware collaborative ensemble learning. *IEEE Transactions on Image Processing (TIP)*. DOI: 10.1109/tip.2020.2998275 25

Ye, Mang, Lan, Xiangyuan, and Yuen, Pong C. (2018). Robust anchor embedding for unsupervised video person re-identification in the wild. In *Proc. of European Conference on Computer Vision*, pages 170–186. DOI: 10.1007/978-3-030-01234-2_11 38

Ye, Mang, Ma, Andy J., Zheng, Liang, Li, Jiawei, and Yuen, Pong C. (2017). Dynamic label graph matching for unsupervised video re-identification. In *Proc. of the IEEE International Conference on Computer Vision*, pages 5142–5150. DOI: 10.1109/iccv.2017.550 6, 30, 31

Ye, Mang, Shen, Jianbing, Lin, Gaojie, Xiang, Tao, Shao, Ling, and Hoi, Steven C. H. (2021). Deep learning for person re-identification: A survey and outlook. *IEEE Transactions on Pattern Analysis and Machine Intelligence*. DOI: 10.1109/tpami.2021.3054775 3

Ye, Mang, Shen, Jianbing, Zhang, Xu, Yuen, Pong C., and Chang, Shih-Fu (2020b). Augmentation invariant and instance spreading feature for softmax embedding. *IEEE TPAMI*. DOI: 10.1109/tpami.2020.3013379 25

Ye, Mang and Yuen, Pong C. (2020). PurifyNet: A robust person re-identification model with noisy labels. *IEEE Transactions on Information Forensics and Security*, 15:2655–2666. DOI: 10.1109/tifs.2020.2970590 25

Yi, Dong, Lei, Zhen, Liao, Shengcai, Li, Stan Z., et al. (2014). Deep metric learning for person re-identification. In *ICPR*. DOI: 10.1109/icpr.2014.16 4

Yu, Hong-Xing, Wu, Ancong, and Zheng, Wei-Shi (2017). Cross-view asymmetric metric learning for unsupervised person re-identification. In *ICCV*, pages 994–1002. DOI: 10.1109/iccv.2017.113 6, 53

Yu, Hong-Xing, Zheng, Wei-Shi, Wu, Ancong, Guo, Xiaowei, Gong, Shaogang, and Lai, Jian-Huang (2019). Unsupervised person re-identification by soft multilabel learning. In *Proc. of the IEEE Conference on Computer Vision and Pattern Recognition*, pages 2148–2157. DOI: 10.1109/cvpr.2019.00225 5, 6

Zagoruyko, Sergey and Komodakis, Nikos (2016). Paying more attention to attention: Improving the performance of convolutional neural networks via attention transfer. *ArXiv Preprint ArXiv:1612.03928*. 57

Zhai, Yunpeng, Ye, Qixiang, Lu, Shijian, Jia, Mengxi, Ji, Rongrong, and Tian, Yonghong (2020). Multiple expert brainstorming for domain adaptive person re-identification. *ArXiv Preprint ArXiv:2007.01546*. DOI: 10.1007/978-3-030-58571-6_35 58

Zhang, Xinyu, Cao, Jiewei, Shen, Chunhua, and You, Mingyu (2019a). Self-training with progressive augmentation for unsupervised cross-domain person re-identification. In *Proc. of the IEEE International Conference on Computer Vision*, pages 8222–8231. DOI: 10.1109/iccv.2019.00831 31

Zhang, Zhizheng, Lan, Cuiling, Zeng, Wenjun, and Chen, Zhibo (2019b). Densely semantically aligned person re-identification. In *Proc. of the IEEE/CVF Conference on Computer Vision and Pattern Recognition*, pages 667–676. DOI: 10.1109/cvpr.2019.00076 4

Zhang, Ziming and Saligrama, Venkatesh (2016). Prism: Person re-identification via structured matching. *IEEE Transactions on Circuits and Systems for Video Technology*, 27(3):499–512. DOI: 10.1109/tcsvt.2016.2596159 31

Zhao, Rui, Ouyang, Wanli, and Wang, Xiaogang (2013). Unsupervised salience learning for person re-identification. In *CVPR*. DOI: 10.1109/cvpr.2013.460 5, 46

Zheng, Liang, Bie, Zhi, Sun, Yifan, Wang, Jingdong, Su, Chi, Wang, Shengjin, and Tian, Qi (2016a). Mars: A video benchmark for large-scale person re-identification. In *European Conference on Computer Vision*, pages 868–884, Springer. DOI: 10.1007/978-3-319-46466-4_52 29, 37

Zheng, Liang, Shen, Liyue, Tian, Lu, Wang, Shengjin, Wang, Jingdong, and Tian, Qi (2015a). Scalable person re-identification: A benchmark. In *ICCV*. DOI: 10.1109/iccv.2015.133 21

Zheng, Liang, Yang, Yi, and Hauptmann, Alexander G. (2016b). Person re-identification: Past, present and future. *ArXiv Preprint ArXiv:1610.02984.* 3

Zheng, Meng, Karanam, Srikrishna, Wu, Ziyan, and Radke, Richard J. (2019). Re-identification with consistent attentive siamese networks. In *Proc. of the IEEE/CVF Conference on Computer Vision and Pattern Recognition*, pages 5735–5744. DOI: 10.1109/cvpr.2019.00588 4

Zheng, Wei-Shi, Gong, Shaogang, and Xiang, Tao (2013). Re-identification by relative distance comparison. *IEEE Transactions on Pattern Analysis and Machine Intelligence*, 35(3):653–668. DOI: 10.1109/tpami.2012.138 4

Zheng, Wei-Shi, Gong, Shaogang, and Xiang, Tao (2016c). Towards open-world person re-identification by one-shot group-based verification. *TPAMI.* DOI: 10.1109/tpami.2015.2453984 7

Zheng, Wei-Shi, Li, Xiang, Xiang, Tao, Liao, Shengcai, Lai, Jianhuang, and Gong, Shaogang (2015b). Partial person re-identification. In *Proc. of the IEEE International Conference on Computer Vision*, pages 4678–4686. DOI: 10.1109/iccv.2015.531 7

Zhong, Zhun, Zheng, Liang, Luo, Zhiming, Li, Shaozi, and Yang, Yi (2019). Invariance matters: Exemplar memory for domain adaptive person re-identification. In *Proc. of the IEEE Conference on Computer Vision and Pattern Recognition*, pages 598–607. DOI: 10.1109/cvpr.2019.00069 5

Zhong, Zhun, Zheng, Liang, Zheng, Zhedong, Li, Shaozi, and Yang, Yi (2018). Camera style adaptation for person re-identification. In *Proc. of the IEEE Conference on Computer Vision and Pattern Recognition*, pages 5157–5166. DOI: 10.1109/cvpr.2018.00541 5

Zhou, Sanping, Wang, Fei, Huang, Zeyi, and Wang, Jinjun (2019). Discriminative feature learning with consistent attention regularization for person re-identification. In *Proc. of the IEEE/CVF International Conference on Computer Vision*, pages 8040–8049. DOI: 10.1109/iccv.2019.00813 4

Zhou, Sanping, Wang, Jinjun, Meng, Deyu, Xin, Xiaomeng, Li, Yubing, Gong, Yihong, and Zheng, Nanning (2018). Deep self-paced learning for person re-identification. *Pattern Recognition*, 76:739–751. DOI: 10.1016/j.patcog.2017.10.005 4

Zhou, Yi and Shao, Ling (2018). Aware attentive multi-view inference for vehicle re-identification. In *Proc. of the IEEE Conference on Computer Vision and Pattern Recognition*, pages 6489–6498. 1

Zhou, Zhen, Huang, Yan, Wang, Wei, Wang, Liang, and Tan, Tieniu (2017). See the forest for the trees: Joint spatial and temporal recurrent neural networks for video-based person re-identification. In *Proc. of the IEEE Conference on Computer Vision and Pattern Recognition*, pages 4747–4756. DOI: 10.1109/cvpr.2017.717 4

Zhou, Zhi-Hua (2018). A brief introduction to weakly supervised learning. *National Science Review*, 5(1):44–53. DOI: 10.1093/nsr/nwx106 2

Zhu, Xiatian, Wu, Botong, Huang, Dongcheng, and Zheng, Wei-Shi (2017). Fast open-world person re-identification. *IEEE Transactions on Image Processing*, 27(5):2286–2300. DOI: 10.1109/tip.2017.2740564 7

Zoph, Barret and Le, Quoc V. (2016). Neural architecture search with reinforcement learning. *ArXiv Preprint ArXiv:1611.01578.* 61

Authors' Biographies

RAMESWAR PANDA

Rameswar Panda obtained his Ph.D. in Electrical and Computer Engineering from University of California, Riverside. Prior to joining UC Riverside, he obtained his M.S. from Jadavpur University and B.E. from Biju Patnaik University of Technology, both in India. While studying for his Ph.D., Rameswar worked at NEC Labs America, Adobe Research, and Siemens Corporate Research. His primary research interests span the areas of computer vision, machine learning, and multimedia. In particular, his current focus is on making AI systems more efficient, i.e., developing novel deep learning methods that can operate with less human-annotated data (data efficient) and less computation (model efficient). He is also interested in image/video understanding, unsupervised/self-supervised representation learning, and multimodal learning (e.g., combining vision, sound/speech and language). His work has been published in top-tier conferences such as CVPR, ICCV, ECCV, NeurIPS, ICML, and ICLR, as well as high impact journals such as *TIP* and *TMM*. He actively participates as a program committee member for many top AI conferences and was leading co-chair of the workshop on Multi-modal Video Analysis at ICCV 2019, ECCV 2020 and Workshop on Neural Architecture Search at CVPR 2020, CVPR 2021.

AMIT K. ROY-CHOWDHURY

Amit K. Roy-Chowdhury received his Ph.D. from the University of Maryland, College Park (UMCP) in 2002 and joined the University of California, Riverside (UCR) in 2004 where he is a Professor and Bourns Family Faculty Fellow of Electrical and Computer Engineering, Director of the Center for Robotics and Intelligent Systems, and Cooperating Faculty in the department of Computer Science and Engineering. He leads the Video Computing Group at UCR, working on foundational principles of computer vision, image processing, and statistical learning, with applications in cyber-physical, autonomous, and intelligent systems. He co-directs the US Department of Defense Center of Excellence NC4: Networked, Configurable Command, Control and Communications for Rapid Situational Awareness. He has published over 200 papers in peer-reviewed journals and conferences, and he is the first author of the book *Camera Networks: The Acquisition and Analysis of Videos Over Wide Areas*. He is on the editorial boards of major journals and program committees of the main conferences in his area. His students have been first authors on multiple papers that received Best Paper Awards at major international conferences, including ICASSP and ICMR. He is a Fellow of the IEEE and IAPR, received the Doctoral

Dissertation Advising/Mentoring Award 2019 from UCR, and the ECE Distinguished Alumni Award from UMCP.

Printed in the United States
by Baker & Taylor Publisher Services